Design Basics

reproduced on the cover
Stuart Davis. *Swing Landscape.* 1938.
Oil on canvas, 7'1½" × 14'5½" (2.17 × 4.41 m).
Indiana University Art Museum, Bloomington.

cover design
Karen Salsgiver

DesignBasics

David A. Lauer

College of Alameda
Alameda, California

Holt, Rinehart and Winston
New York   Chicago   San Francisco
Atlanta   Dallas   Montreal   Toronto
London   Sydney

For my
father and mother,
who would have
been pleased.

Editor: Rita Gilbert
Picture Editor: Joan Curtis
Developmental Editor: Patricia Gallagher
Production Assistants: Barbara Curialle, Laura Foti
Production Supervisor: Robert de Villeneuve
Illustrator: Sandra E. Popovich
Designer: Karen Salsgiver

Illustration **a**, page 102, from *Photography: A Handbook of History, Materials, and Process* by Charles Swedlund. Copyright © 1974 by Holt, Rinehart and Winston, Inc.

Illustration **a**, page 122, from *Ten Ever-Lovin' Blue-Eyed Years With Pogo* by Walt Kelly. Copyright © 1959 by Walt Kelly. Reprinted by permission of Simon & Schuster, a Division of Gulf & Western Corporation.

Library of Congress Cataloging in Publication Data

Lauer, David A.
  Design basics.

  Bibliography: p. 234
  Includes index.
  1. Design. I Title.
NK1510.L38   745.4   78-10766
ISBN 0-03-043611-7

Composition and camera work by York Graphic
  Services, Inc., Pennsylvania
Color separations and printing by Lehigh Press
  Lithographers, New Jersey
Printing and binding by Capital City Press, Vermont
123   138   876

Preface

Design Basics is an introductory text for studio classes in two-dimensional design. It presents the fundamental elements and principles of design—as they relate to drawing, painting, and the graphic arts—in a flexible format that lends itself to many different teaching approaches.

Instructors generally recognize the importance of a course in basic design as the foundation for all a student's future work in art. Many students, however, have difficulty with this course and feel the need for a textbook, an overall reference guide, to give them a framework in which to learn. It was to fulfill this need for my own students that *Design Basics* was originally conceived.

It seems that no two designers will ever agree on the same list of design elements and principles—nor on which are which. For this book I have focused upon: unity, emphasis/focal point, balance, scale/proportion, line, form, texture, illusion of space, illusion of motion, rhythm, and color. The list is arranged in a strictly personal sequence. It is customary in "art appreciation" courses to present the elements first. But for a studio class, this is backward. The student is actually creating design projects immediately, so the principles of organization are more fundamental than the particular element involved.

Actually, in *Design Basics* the order of presentation is inconsequential. I have deliberately organized the book so that it can be used in any sequence desired. Each individual topic is dealt with in a self-contained two-page spread, where the reader will find all the discussion and illustrations relating to that topic. There are no cross-references, and no discussion depends upon information gleaned in another part of the text. The student can open the book anywhere and find a complete statement about the subject in question. *Design Basics*, therefore, should serve as an easy-to-use reference work. All explanations are written in simple, clear language; insofar as possible, I have avoided artistic jargon.

The discussion in *Design Basics* is supported by two types of illustrations. The first are simple, abstract designs—nonobjective patterns of shapes, lines, and textures—created especially for this book. They relate to the kinds of projects the students will be working on. The second category includes drawings, paintings, prints, and graphics by master artists, past and present. These are meant to demonstrate that the very same artistic ideas and principles can be applied to much more complicated images—and have been so applied by all artists, sophisticated or untutored, through the centuries. In the final chapter, dealing with color, virtually all the illustrations are presented in four-color reproduction.

Because this is a working text, illustrations are identified only by code letters, although a documenting caption in small type also appears on the page. The reader is not studying artists, stylistic development, themes, or historical periods. The pictures serve a teaching purpose different from that in an art history text.

It is not my intention to replace the design instructor. Each topic in *Design Basics* is dealt with only briefly, with a few clear pictorial examples. The instructor undoubtedly will want to give a more thorough explanation and more illustrations. The aim of the book, then, is to *reinforce* the instructor's presentation, not supplant it, and to provide material for student reference later. For this reason, there are no assignments or projects given in the book. I feel that assignments are the province of the instructor and can be developed most effectively in the context of a given class.

A design text should teach by example as well as by words. I have planned *Design Basics* to show the kind of clean, uncluttered format and layout that should represent the subject matter at its best.

Acknowledgments

Many people have helped in the preparation of *Design Basics*, but I must give special thanks to Ernest B. Ball and Richard L. Falk for their suggestions and encouragement throughout the long process of making a book. I am also indebted to Donna K. Westerman, of Orange Coast College; Cory Millican, of Cornell University; Peter A. Slusarski, of Kent State University; Douglas DeVinny, of Mesa College; and Nicholas von Bujdoss, of Smith College—all of whom read the first draft of my manuscript and offered constructive criticism.

For the staff at Holt, Rinehart and Winston I reserve my most glowing thanks. "Without whom this book could not have been written" sounds trite, but it applies exactly to my editor, Rita Gilbert, and to picture editor Joan Curtis. Together, they took my adequate efforts and turned them into what I feel is truly a fine book. At the same time, I cannot ignore the contributions of developmental editor Patricia Gallagher, and her assistants Barbara Curialle and Laura Foti, who managed to hold together all the thousands of elements involved in an art book. Last is first, and I owe special gratitude to designer Karen Salsgiver for giving concrete—and elegant—form to my conviction that a design book should teach by example.

San Francisco   D. A. L.
October 1978

Contents

Design Basics

Unity

1

Unity

Unity, the presentation of a unified image, is perhaps as close to a "rule" as art approaches. Unity implies that a congruity or agreement exists among the elements in a design; they *look* as though they belong together, as though there is some visual connection beyond mere chance that has caused them to come together. Another term for the same idea is *harmony*. If the various elements are not harmonious, if they appear separate and/or unrelated, your pattern falls apart and lacks unity.

Example **a** illustrates the idea. The harmony or unity of the elements shown results not merely from our recognizing all of them as varieties of scissors. If we had never before seen a pair of scissors, knew nothing of their use in cutting, or even had no name whatever for these forms, we would still notice a certain similarity among them. Despite obvious differences, they have in common enough basic visual characteristics that seem to relate them.

The aim of unity is to make your design coherent and readable. To take the term "readable" in a literal sense for a minute, look at the three versions of the printed word UNITY **(b)**. The first pattern of letters is easy to read and coherent. The second is still organized and readable, even though the letters themselves are now in different sizes and styles of type. In the third example, however, we have difficulty making any sense out of the pattern or seeing the relationship among the elements. The design is confused and fragmented. Of course, in arranging letter forms into word patterns the possibilities are much more limited than in using purely visual design elements, but the underlying idea is comparable.

This should not be cause for alarm. The designer's job is not necessarily difficult. In fact, the viewer *looks* for some organization, something to unify the different elements. The viewer does not *want* to see unrelated chaos. As the designer, you must provide some clues, but the viewer is already searching for some coherent unity. In creating unified designs, your problem starts with picking the elements you wish to combine, but the challenge is truly more in the organization of elements into a composition. Your idea or theme, or even absence of one, does not limit you. It is the artistic skill of organization (or *design*) that produces a unified pattern.

a The units of this design have characteristics in common, despite obvious differences in appearance.

b A design must be coherent in order to be understood.

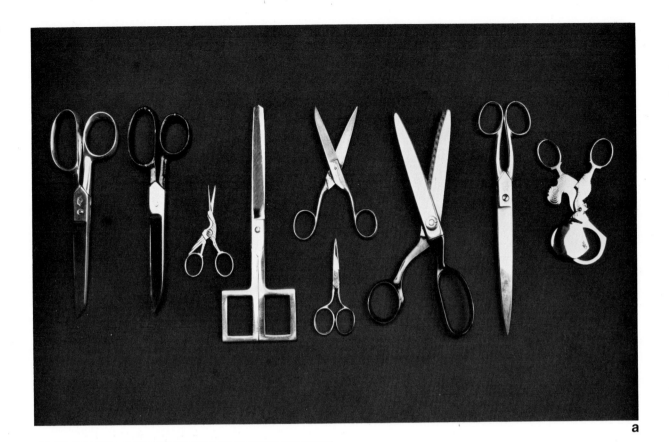

a

Unity

Unity

Unity

b

Unity

An important aspect of visual unity is that the whole must be predominant over the parts; you must first see the *whole* pattern before noticing the individual elements. Each item may have a meaning and certainly add to the total effect, but the viewer must first see the pattern as a whole, rather than simply a collection of unrelated bits and pieces.

This concept differentiates a design from the usual scrapbook page, such as the one in **a**. In a scrapbook, each item is meant to be observed and studied individually, to be enjoyed and then forgotten as your eye moves on to the next souvenir. The result may be interesting, but it is not a unified design.

Do not confuse *intellectual unity* with *visual unity*. Visual unity denotes some harmony or agreement between the items that is apparent to the *eye*. To say that a scrapbook page is "unified" because all the items have a common theme (your family, your wedding, your vacation at the beach) is unity by *idea*—that is, a conceptual unity not observable by the eye. A unifying *idea* will not necessarily produce a unified pattern.

In **b** the scrapbook items have been organized so that we are aware first of the total pattern they make together, and then afterwards we

begin to enjoy the items separately. Example **b** is a unified design. Here, as is often the case, in creating a design the actual elements chosen are less important than what the artist does with them.

The need for visual unity does not deny that there can be an intellectual pleasure in design as well. Harmony of idea and visual symbol is certainly important. In **c** the visual unity results from the horizontal movement of both the lettering and the illustration. However, the intellectual connection of the word "mummies" with the picture of an embalmed hand that replaces the usual pointing finger symbol gives added enjoyment. In **d** the repetition of horizontal elements centered on a common axis provides visual unity. But much of our interest is intellectual and comes from recognizing the familiar Red Cross symbol now only "half full" in reference to blood donations.

a If a pattern does not have unity, it remains simply a collection of fragments.
b Organizing the different units into a pattern results in a coherent design.
c *To the Mummies.* Poster for the Museum of Fine Arts, Boston. Art director and designer, Ken Amaral; writer, Peter H. Caroline; photographer, Phil Porcella; agency, Humphrey, Browning, and MacDougall, Boston.
d *We're Running Out.* Poster for the American Red Cross, Cleveland Chapter. Art director and designer, Don Ozyp; agency, Griswold-Eshleman, Cleveland.

a   **b**

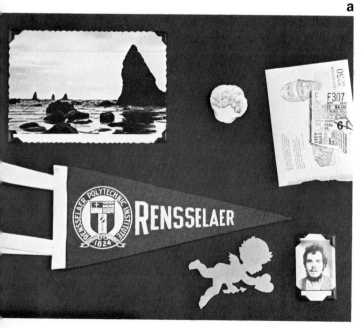

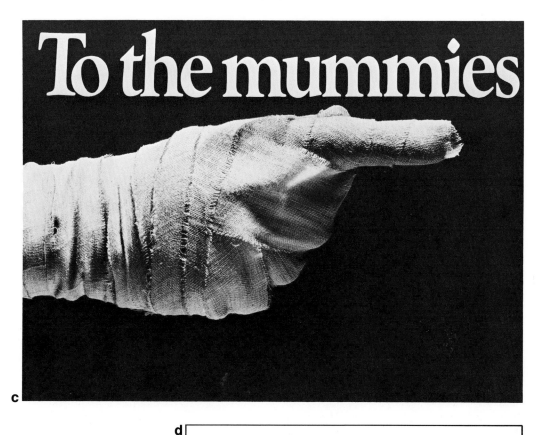

c

d

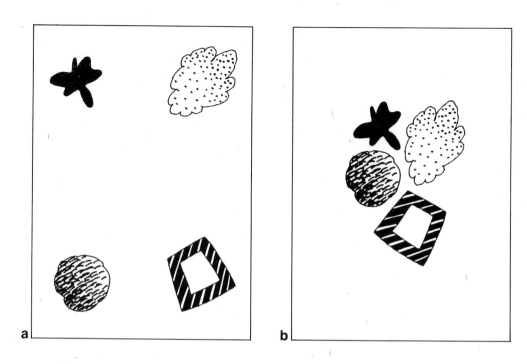

a

b

c

Proximity

An easy way to gain unity—to make separate elements look as if they belong together—is by *proximity*, or simply putting these elements close together. The four elements in **a** appear isolated, as floating bits with no relationship to each other. By putting them close together **(b)**, we begin to see them as a total, related pattern. Proximity is a common unifying factor. By it we recognize constellations in the skies and in fact are able to read. Change the proximity scheme that makes letters into words, and reading is impossible.

In El Greco's painting **(c)** there is a large amount of stormy, though essentially negative, empty space. The smaller nude figures, however, do not float haphazardly in the turbulent background. Instead, they are grouped together making a horizontal unit across the painting. Arms and legs reach out to touch adjoining fig-ures, so that the bodies come together. The drapery on the ground also unites the saint's figure with those behind.

Example **d** shows a portrait by Henri de Toulouse-Lautrec. The objects on the table seem an apparently casual collection of items, but by their pattern of proximity they make a coherent design. The eye is led carefully from one thing to another by the way they are positioned and almost touch at times. And, finally, the wine carafe leads the eye away and up to the seated figures.

a If they are isolated from one another, elements appear unrelated.
b Placing elements near each other enables us to see them in a pattern.
c El Greco. *The Vision of St. John the Divine.* 1608–14. Oil on canvas, 7′4½″ × 6′4″ (2.25 × 1.93 m). Metropolitan Museum of Art, New York (Rogers Fund, 1956).
d Henri de Toulouse-Lautrec. *Monsieur Boileau at the Café.* 1893. Gouache on cardboard, 31½ × 25½″ (80 × 65 cm). Cleveland Museum of Art (Hinman B. Hurlbut Collection).

Unity

Repetition

A most valuable and widely used device for achieving visual unity is *repetition*. As the term implies, it simply means that something repeats in various parts of the design to relate those parts together. The element that repeats may be almost anything: a color, a shape, a texture, a direction or angle, and so forth. In a lithograph by Robert Rauschenberg **(a)** the repetition is very apparent; indeed, the two outermost forms are almost identical. But all the forms repeat some visual characteristics: the rectangles with a triangular top, the texture of various wrapping papers and tapes, and the bits of type and lettering that reappear. The forms all seem related to each other.

Repetition of shape is also evident in Picasso's painting, *The Studio* **(b)**. Rectangles, triangles, and circles repeat, and in addition we can find an amazing number of parallel diagonals. The simplification of natural shapes into geometric abstractions makes Picasso's process of repetition fairly obvious to the eye.

Abstraction, however, is not required for repetition. In Degas' *The Millinery Shop* **(c)** notice how often the artist repeats a circle motif—the hats, the flowers and bows, the lady's head, bosom, and skirt. The painting is a whole design of circles broken by a few verticals (the hat stands, the ribbons, the back draperies) and a triangle or so (the table, the bent arm, and the front hat's ribbons). When we look beyond the subject matter in art, we begin to see the artist's use of repetition to create a sense of unity. Color is the element most commonly used for repetition and unity; in fact, finding artworks where colors *do not* repeat would be quite difficult.

a Robert Rauschenberg. *Tampa 2.* 1973. Three-color lithograph and blueprint, 2'5½" × 6'2½" (.75 × 1.89 m). Courtesy Graphicstudio, University of South Florida, Tampa.
b Pablo Picasso. *The Studio.* 1927-28. Oil on canvas, 4'11" × 7'7" (1.5 × 2.31 m). Museum of Modern Art, New York (gift of Walter P. Chrysler, Jr.).
c Edgar Degas. *The Millinery Shop.* 1882. Oil on canvas, 39⅛" × 43⅜" (99 × 110 cm). Art Institute of Chicago (Mr. and Mrs. Lewis L. Coburn Memorial Collection).

a

b

c

Unity

Continuation

A third way to achieve unity is by *continuation*, a more subtle device than proximity or repetition, which are fairly obvious. Continuation, naturally, means something "continues"—usually a line, an edge, or a direction from one form to another. The viewer's eye is carried smoothly from one element to another by their careful placement of just touching or continuous contour from one to the next.

The design in **a** is unified by the closeness and the character of the elements. In **b**, though, the shapes seem even more a unit, since they are arranged in such a way that one's eye flows easily from one element to the next. The shapes no longer float casually. They are now organized into a definite, set pattern.

In the pastel drawing by Degas **(c)** a minute's study reveals many places where the eye is carried from one form to another by placement. The line of the round tub starts at the bather's hairline, meets her fingertips, and joins the vertical line of the shelf where the brush handle overlaps. The circular shape of the bather's hips is just tangent to the same shelf edge. Notice the careful arrangement of the objects on the shelf—how each item barely touches or carries the eye to another. That at first glance the arrangement seemed casual and unplanned only adds to our admiration for the artist.

The early Irish manuscript page in **d** shows many places where the large decorative initial letter, the words of the text, and the incredibly ornate areas of border patterns are visually united by placement for continuation. The various elements "fit" together to form a unit, and our eyes move easily from one part to another.

a Proximity and similarity unify a design.
b The unity of the same design is intensified when the elements are brought into contact with each other in a continuing line.
c Edgar Degas. *The Tub*. 1886. Pastel, 23½ × 32⅓″ (60 × 82 cm). Louvre, Paris.
d Initial page from the Lindisfarne Gospels. c. 700. The British Library, London (reproduced by permission of the British Library Board).

a

b

c

d

Unity

Design implies unity—a harmonious pattern or order established among the various elements. However, it is possible to make a pattern so highly unified that the result, instead of being visual satisfaction, rather quickly becomes visual boredom. The checkerboard design in **a** is an example. With its scrupulous use of proximity, constant repetition, and careful lining up of the elements, the design is assuredly an excellent example of unity—and also quite a dull thing to look at. The designer's aim is to achieve unity, but a unity that branches out into variations that relieve boredom. *Unity with variety* is the oft-quoted artistic ideal, or *theme and variations* as the idea is so aptly called in music. Shapes may repeat but perhaps in different sizes; colors may repeat but perhaps in different values, and so forth. The easiest way to explain will be to look at examples.

The Mondrian painting **(b)** in many ways resembles the checkerboard, but how much more visually interesting it is. This interest comes basically from an application of the unity-with-variety principle. The varying sizes and shapes of the rectangles, the subtle changes in the thickness of the black lines, the placement

of a few colored shapes, the delicate variations of horizontal and vertical emphasis—all these serve to maintain our interest far longer than the checkerboard.

Variety is necessary in all types of designs, not only in abstract patterns such as the Mondrian. In Vermeer's painting **(c)** an almost endless variety of rectangles can be found framing and emphasizing the different-sized and colored circular forms on and around the central subject.

The quilted tapestry **(d)** has a unity based on repetition of triangular shapes. A great deal of variety is introduced: the triangles are different sizes, and the colors and patterns of the many materials vary. Notice how the lines of the stitching reinforce the triangle theme and, in effect, create countless more triangles.

a Unity without variety can result in a monotonous design.
b Piet Mondrian. *Rhythm of Straight Lines.* 1936–42.
Oil on canvas, 28¼ × 27″ (71 × 69 cm). Private collection.
c Jan Vermeer. *The Love Letter.* 1666. Oil on canvas,
17¼ × 15¼″ (44 × 39 cm). Rijksmuseum, Amsterdam.
d Susan Hoffman. *Invention in the Spirit of J. S. Bach.* 1975.
Quilted tapestry, 7′9″ × 6′10″ (2.36 × 2.08 m).
Courtesy Kornblee Gallery, New York.

a

b

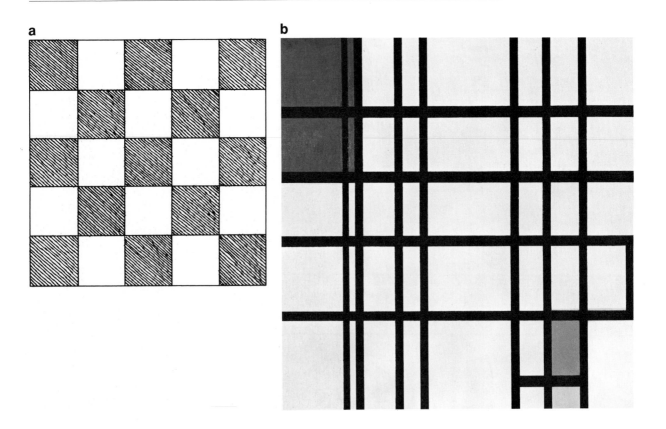

c

d

a

b

Unity

Architectural designs reveal a similar concern for unity with variety. The Farnese Palace in Rome **(a)** shows the principle clearly. Countless rectangles are organized in a coherent manner, with the pattern of the windows employing continuation both horizontally and vertically. Notice that the above-the-window (or pediment) treatment varies in each story: sometimes flat, sometimes rounded, sometimes triangular, and, on the upper story, triangular without a base. The central curved crest clearly becomes a focal point, leading the eye to the large arched doorway, which itself repeats the other smaller curved elements. The façade is highly unified, the variety restrained and subtle. As a result, the building is dignified and imposing, its stateliness proclaimed immediately by its design.

Dignified austerity is certainly not a feature of Little Moreton Hall **(b)**. As a structure, it has none of the logical overall planning that went into the Farnese Palace. Extensions, rooms, and wings were added progressively by succeeding generations of the family, so that a complicated higgledy-piggledy structure results. However, the decoration functions as the unifying factor. The timber-and-plaster construction (the English Tudor *half-timbered* or *black-and-white* style) unifies all the extensions into a harmonious whole. But variety still asserts itself—and what marvelous variety! Each addition continues the basic black-and-white design pattern, but each wing, often each floor, gives us new patterns, new motifs, and slight but definite variations.

Unity with variety is apparent in a Greek village **(c)** where the similarity of the structures is broken only by uneven streets and alleyways.

a Antonio da Sangallo and Michelangelo. Farnese Palace, Rome. 1530–39.
b Little Moreton Hall, Cheshire, England. c. 1559–89.
c View of the island of Serifos, Greece.

c

Unity

Is the principle of *unity with variety* a conscious, planned ingredient supplied by the artist or designer, or is it something that a confident designer produces automatically? There is no real answer. The only certain thing is that the principle can be seen in art from every different period, culture, and geographic area.

Kandinsky's painting **(a)** is titled *Several Circles, No. 323.* The decision to create a composition unified by the repetition of circles was clearly an initial and deliberate choice by the artist. The changes in size, color, and value of the various circles must also have been purposeful, because these changes provide the interest of variety to the painting.

The piece of tapa cloth **(b)** done by a native of Samoa is another matter. No art school or textbook taught this artist anything about unity with variety, yet the design shows it so markedly. Each horizontal band contains similar linear elements with triangles and arrows repeated over and over. But the sizes vary, and each area combines the elements in a different manner.

There must be an intuitive satisfaction that does not have to be taught in the idea of related variations. The ceremonial house decoration from New Guinea **(c)** shows this principle employed by an untutored, "primitive" artist.

A conscious use of unity with variety does not necessarily lessen our pleasure as viewers. From the entrance foyer at Newby Hall **(d)** we can see that the same radial design pattern has been repeated in different ways, not only in the Adam-designed plaster ceiling and the marble floor, but even in the backs of the specially made Chippendale chairs. This is certainly contrived, but nonetheless delightful.

a Wassily Kandinsky. *Several Circles, No. 323.* 1926. Oil on canvas, 4'7⅛" (1.4 m) square. Solomon R. Guggenheim Museum, New York.
b Tapa cloth, from Samoa, 5'6" × 3'4" (1.68 × 1.02 m). American Museum of Natural History, New York.
c *Hornbill,* ceremonial house decoration from Abelam, New Guinea. Wood and paint, height 44¼" (112 cm). Metropolitan Museum of Art, New York (Michael C. Rockefeller Memorial Collection of Primitive Art).
d Robert Adam. Entrance Hall at Newby Hall, Yorkshire, England. c. 1780. From *Newby Hall: An Illustrated Survey of the Yorkshire Home of the Compton Family* (English Life Publications, Ltd.).

a

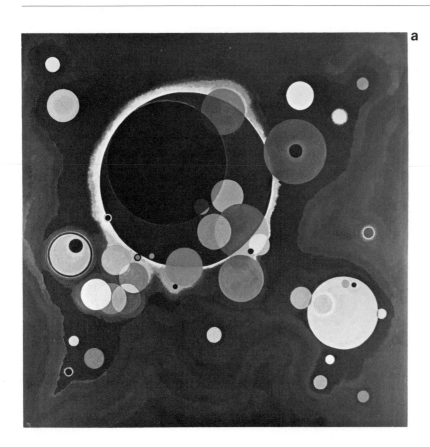

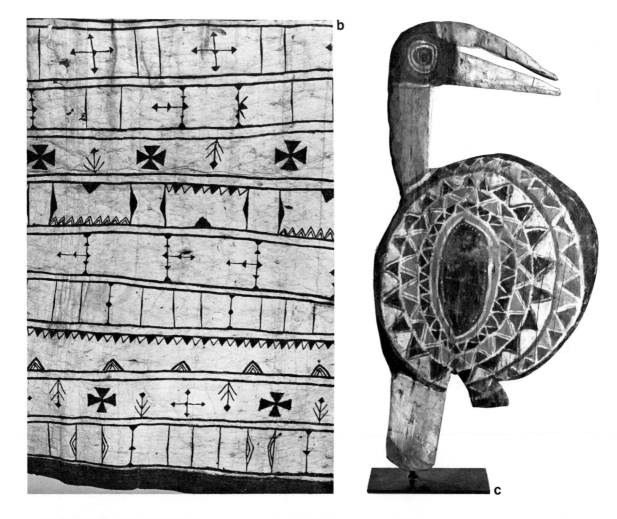

b

c

d

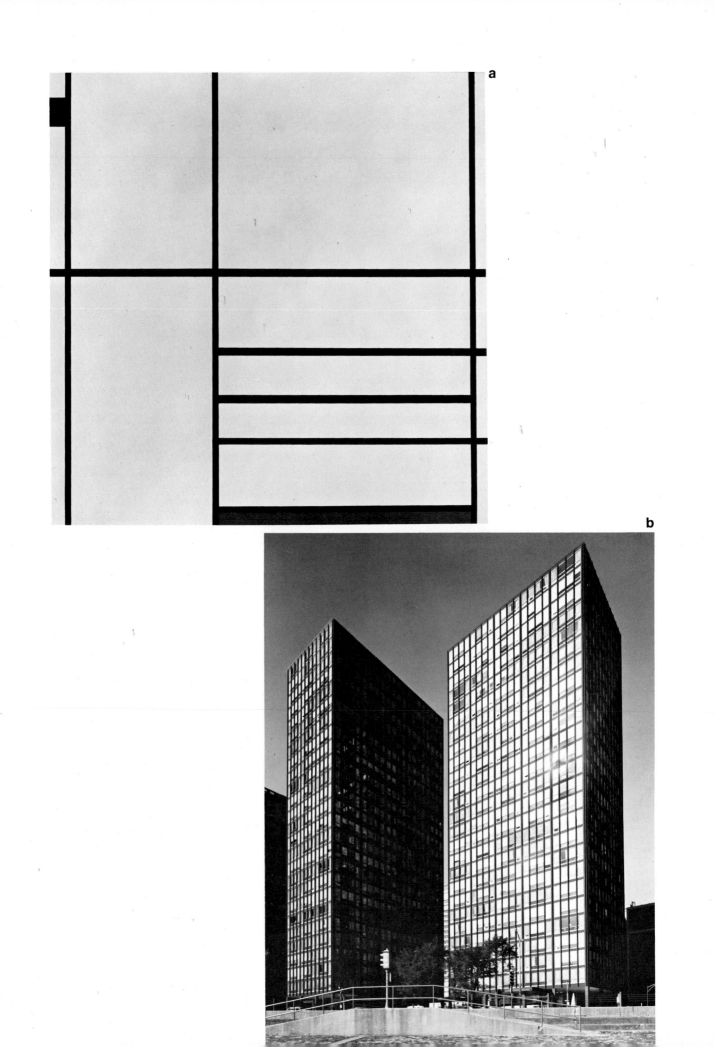

a

b

Unity

Unity with variety does create a pleasant visual sensation. The general public uses this principle as a critical basis on looking at art, despite the fact that many people have never heard or read the phrase.

Paintings such as Mondrian's **(a)** are often criticized by the lay observer for being "too dull," "too intellectual," and "boring! nothing there." How often we hear such buildings as the ones in **b** termed "cold," "sterile," and "too antiseptic." In both cases what the various comments truly mean is that the designs have an overwhelming unity, but the variety is so subtle as to be insufficient for that particular viewer's taste.

In galleries or museums, when expressionist abstractions such as **c** are exhibited, one constantly overhears criticisms such as: "I don't like it—too messy"; or: "too wild and uncontrolled"; and even: "My two-year-old could do *that*." What these self-styled critics are saying is

that the variety in such a picture is extremely obvious, but their eyes cannot discern any sense of order or unity imposed on that variety. The scales have tipped too far in one direction for them.

The "correct" balance between unity and variety—between control and spontaneous freedom—varies with the individual artist, with the theme or purpose, and eventually with the viewer. The only "rule" seems to be that both qualities must be present. The complete absence of one or the other is definitely unsatisfactory. Utter boredom or utter confusion result, and neither is visually desirable.

a Piet Mondrian. *Composition in White, Black, and Red.* 1936. Oil on canvas, 40¼ × 41″ (102 × 104 cm). Museum of Modern Art, New York (gift of the Advisory Committee).
b Ludwig Miës van der Rohe. Lake Shore Apartments, Chicago. 1950-52.
c Jackson Pollock. *Mural on Indian Red Ground.* 1950. Oil and enamel on canvas mounted on board, 6 × 8′ (1.83 × 2.44 m). Tehran Museum of Contemporary Art.

c

Emphasis / Focal Point

Emphasis/Focal Point

The designer's main enemy is boredom. It is almost better for viewers to stand and revile your image, rather than to pass it quickly with a bored "ho-hum." Your job is to catch attention and provide a pattern that stimulates the viewer by offering some visual satisfaction. Nothing will guarantee success, but one device that can help is a point of emphasis, a *focal point*. This attracts attention and encourages the viewer to look further.

In a picture or design with a story to tell, the viewer can be shown immediately, "Here is the most important character or element." In **a**, entitled *John Brown Going to His Hanging*, the American artist Horace Pippin carefully points out the figure of John Brown. He is the first thing we see. The dark figure is somewhat isolated from the other elements and is silhouetted against the light building. The wagon, the other figures, and even the tree trunks and branches frame the focal point.

Even in purely abstract or nonobjective patterns, a focal point will attract the viewer's eye and give some contrast and visual excitement. The **V** shape in the center of Kline's painting **(b)** is a brilliant yellow. This light element stands out against the dark shapes and immediately establishes the feeling of dynamic movement that permeates the composition.

There need not be only one focal point, but the designer must be careful not to provide too many. As in a three-ring circus, the viewer does not know where to look first, and confusion replaces interest. When *everything* is emphasized, *nothing* is emphasized.

a Horace Pippin. *John Brown Going to His Hanging.* 1942. Oil on canvas, 24 × 30″ (59 × 79 cm). Pennsylvania Academy of Fine Arts, Philadelphia.
b Franz Kline. *King Oliver.* 1958. Oil on canvas, 8′3″ × 6′5½″ (2.51 × 1.97 m). Collection Mr. and Mrs. I. Donald Grossman, New York.

a

b

Emphasis/Focal Point

Very often in art the pictorial emphasis is clear, and in simple compositions (such as a portrait) the focal point is obvious. But the more complicated the pattern, the more necessary or helpful a focal point may become in organizing the design.

As a general rule, a focal point results when one element differs from the others. Whatever interrupts an overall feeling or pattern automatically attracts the eye by this very difference. The possibilities are almost endless:

- When most of the elements are vertical, the few horizontal forms break the pattern and become focal points.
- When most elements are irregular, spontaneous forms, an almost geometric square shape breaks the pattern and becomes the focal point **(a)**.
- In a design consisting mainly of flat planes of color, a detailed, linear, multicolored area is emphasized **(b)**.

Emphasis by Contrast

- When many elements are about the same size and one is much larger, that one element is visually important **(c)**.
- When natural forms are highly distorted, the occasional recognizable part becomes an immediate focus of attention **(d)**.

The list could go on and on; many other possibilities will occur to you. Sometimes this idea is called *emphasis by contrast*. The element that contrasts with, rather than continuing, the prevailing design scheme becomes the focal point.

a Sam Francis. *Facing Within.* 1975. Acrylic on canvas, 5′6″ × 7′ (1.68 × 2.13 m). Courtesy André Emmerich Gallery, New York.
b Georges Braque. *Musical Forms* (or *Guitar and Clarinet*). 1918. Pasted paper, corrugated cardboard, charcoal, and gouache on cardboard; 30⅜ × 37⅜″ (77 × 95 cm). Philadelphia Museum of Art (Louise and Walter Arensberg Collection).
c *Emperor Otto II*, from the *Registrum Gregorii.* Trier, c. 985. Manuscript illumination, 10⅝ × 7⅞″ (27 × 20 cm). Musée Condé, Chantilly.
d Lucas Samaras. *Photo-Transformation.* 1974. Polaroid SX-70 manipulation of photoemulsion pigments, 3″ (8 cm) square. Courtesy Pace Gallery, New York.

a

b

c

d

Emphasis/Focal Point

Emphasis by Isolation

A variation on the device of emphasis by contrast is the useful technique of *emphasis by isolation*. When one item is isolated or sits apart from the other elements or groups of elements, it becomes a focal point. Just by its separation alone, an element takes on visual importance. This *is* contrast of course, but it is contrast of placement, not form. In such a case, the element need not be any different from the others. The black square in **a** is like others in the design; but its placement away from them draws the eye, and it becomes the focal point.

In the still life by Cézanne **(b)** the pitcher at left repeats the color of the bowl and the cloth, and the design on it repeats the fruit forms. In short, it is part of a unified composition, but it gains visual importance because it sits away from the items grouped together at right. The pitcher is an emphasized element only through its detached position.

Emphasis by Isolation

John Trumbull leaves no room for doubt about the point of emphasis in his painting **(c)**. We cannot miss the generals isolated in the middle, with Washington silhouetted against the sky.

Putting the focal point directly in the center does look a bit contrived. However, it is wise to remember that if a focal point is placed too close to an edge, it will have a tendency to pull the viewer's eye right out of the picture.

a Isolating an element draws our attention to it.
b Paul Cézanne. *Still Life with Apples and Peaches.* c. 1905. Oil on canvas, 32 × 39⅜″ (81 × 100 cm). National Gallery of Art, Washington, D.C. (gift of Eugene and Agnes Meyer, 1959).
c John Trumbull. *Surrender of Lord Cornwallis.* 1787-94. Oil on canvas, 20⅞ × 30⅝″ (53 × 78 cm). Collection Yale University Art Gallery, New Haven, Conn.

a

b

c

Emphasis/Focal Point

The placement of elements in a design may function in another way to create emphasis. If many elements point at one item, our attention is directed there, and a focal point results. A radial design is a perfect example of this device. Just as all forms radiate out from the convergent focus, so they also repeatedly lead our eyes back to this central element. As **a** illustrates, this central element may be just like other forms in the design; the emphasis results from the placement, not from any difference in character of the form itself.

Radial designs are more common in architecture than in two-dimensional art. The more subtle variation in painting occurs when many figures *look* (or sometimes point) in a common direction. In life when we see someone staring or pointing a certain way, we have an almost uncontrollable urge to look there. This happens in art, too. In Curry's scene of a fundamentalist baptism by immersion **(b)** all the figures look directly at the preacher and the girl, automatically directing our eyes there as well. Even the lines of the windmill and the rooflines of

the barn and house direct our eyes to the focal point of these two figures.

In the photograph shown in **c**, the placement is important for emphasis. The two small figures attract attention by their isolation in a large space. Beyond this, their placement at the point where all the lines of the background shapes and the perspective diagonals converge reinforces their dramatic emphasis.

The effect need not necessarily be as obvious as these examples illustrate. A point to remember, however, is that once your focal point has been decided upon, it is wise to avoid having other major or visually important elements point or lead the eye *away* from it. Confusion of emphasis can result.

a Our eyes are drawn to the central element of this design by all the other radiating elements.
b John Steuart Curry. *Baptism in Kansas.* 1928. Oil on canvas, 3'4" × 4'2" (1.02 × 1.27 m). Whitney Museum of American Art, New York.
c Harry Callahan. *Eleanor and Barbara, Chicago 1953.* Photograph. Courtesy Light Gallery, New York.

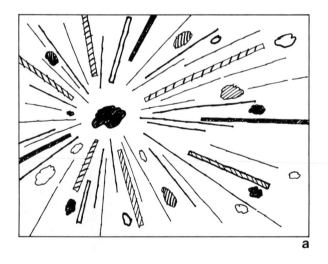

a

b

c

a

b

Emphasis/Focal Point

Degree of Emphasis

In discussing the creation and use of a focal point, a word of warning is in order. There is no real difficulty in introducing a new, contrasting element into a design. However, any emphasis must be created with some subtlety and sense of restraint. The focal point must still remain a part of the overall design, rather than becoming an alien element that looks totally out of place. Imagine a design of soft, grayish-blue squares with one enormous brilliant orange circle. The focal point is obvious, indeed *so* obvious it may overwhelm the rest of the design completely. The viewer's eye certainly sees the focal point, but because this point has overpowering dominance, the eye never leaves it to see the rest of the design.

In Juan Gris' Cubist still life **(a)** the massed group of circles defining the bunch of grapes is a focal point. But the colors of this element are repeated in several other places, and some other small circular forms appear individually elsewhere. The focal point is not a completely unrelated element.

In Degas' painting **(b)**, the isolated ballet dancer at left makes a strong focal point but still remains a part of the total pattern. Though isolated, she repeats other elements in form and color, and various items, such as the dancers' barre, the chair, and the fan, make our eyes connect her with the group at right. See the difference in **c**, where the isolated black shape seems quite unconnected (and too dominant) for the subtle, semicircular elements at the right.

The principle of unity, the creation of a harmonious pattern with related elements, is more important than the injection of a focal point if this point jeopardizes the design's unity.

a Juan Gris. *Bottle, Glass and Fruit Dish.* 1921. Oil on canvas, 24 × 20″ (61 × 50 cm). Kunstmuseum, Basel (Emanuel Hoffmann Foundation).
b Edgar Degas. *The Dance Foyer at the Opéra, rue le Peletier.* 1872. Oil on canvas, 12⅞ × 18½″ (33 × 47 cm). Louvre, Paris.
c Too much emphasis detracts from the unity of a design.

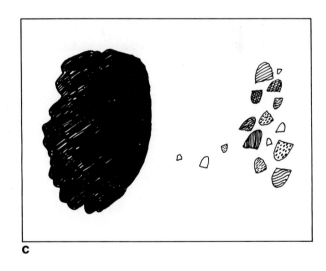

c

Emphasis/Focal Point

Absence of Focal Point

A definite focal point is assuredly not a necessity in creating a successful design. It is a tool that artists may or may not use depending on their aims. Many paintings have rather ambiguous emphasis, and different viewers will see different elements as the most important. Indeed, many artists have purposely ignored the whole idea of a focal point. Warhol's painting of soup cans **(a)** is an example. Here the monotonous repetition of an unaesthetic, commercial image, without the visual relief of any change or emphasis, makes a subtle comment on culture in the United States. The theme really dictates the design pattern.

Similarly, Pollock's huge painting *Number 1* **(b)** is an abstract expression of energy and furious activity. The same twisting, busy labyrinth of complicated lines extends over the whole can-

vas without any real starting point or visual climax to the painting.

Some art forms by their very nature rule out the use of a focal point. Woven and printed fabrics **(c)** generally have no focal point, but instead consist of an unstressed repetition of a motif over the whole surface. A focal point on draperies, bedspreads, or upholstery might be distracting. In clothing, the focal point is provided by the design of the garment.

a Andy Warhol. *100 Soup Cans.* 1962. Casein on canvas. 6' × 4'4" (1.82 × 1.32 m). Collection Karl Ströher, Darmstadt, West Germany.
b Jackson Pollock. *Number 1.* 1948. Oil on canvas, 5'8" × 8'8" (1.73 × 2.64 m). Museum of Modern Art, New York (purchase).
c Tricia Guild. *Fossils.* Printed cotton. Courtesy Braunschweig & Fils, Inc., New York.

a

b

c

Balance

3

Balance

Almost everybody recognizes the building in **a**. However, relatively few people could tell you its architect, its century of construction, or its architectural style. Nevertheless, it is universally famous, and famous for only one distinctive feature: it leans. Indeed, we never speak of it without referring to it as the *Leaning* Tower of Pisa. "Leaning," of course, refers to the fact that it is off balance, a feature almost unique in our knowledge of architecture. Items that are off balance usually right themselves or fall. This tower, doing neither, is world-renowned.

A sense of balance is innate; as children we develop a sense of balance in our bodies and observe balance in the world around us. Lack of balance or *imbalance* disturbs us. Dangerously leaning trees, rocks, furniture, ladders, and so forth are avoided carefully. But even where no physical danger is present, as in a design or painting, we still feel more comfortable with a balanced pattern **(b)**.

In assessing pictorial balance, we always assume a center, vertical axis **(c)** and usually expect to see some kind of equal weight (visual weight) distribution on either side. This axis functions as the fulcrum on a scale or see-saw, and the two sides should achieve a sense of equilibrium. When this equilibrium is not present, as in **d**, a certain vague uneasiness or dissatisfaction results. We feel a need to rearrange the elements, in the same way that we automatically straighten a picture on the wall or a dangerously tilting ladder.

a Bonanno da Pisa. Bell Tower of the Cathedral at Pisa. Begun 1174.
b Giotto. *Madonna Enthroned.* c. 1310. Panel, 10'8" × 6'8" (3.25 × 2.03 m). Uffizi, Florence.
c Balance implies an equal distribution of visual weight.
d An unbalanced design leaves the viewer with a vague uneasiness.

a

b

c

d

Balance

Balance—some sort of equal distribution of visual weight—is a universal aim of composition. The vast majority of pictures we see have been consciously balanced by the artist. However, this does not mean there is no place in art for purposeful imbalance. An artist may, because of a particular theme or topic, expressly desire that a picture raise uneasy, disquieting responses in the viewer. In this instance, imbalance can be a useful tool. Even without such a motive, the occasional almost imbalanced image such as the Japanese print **(a)** does intrigue us and attract our attention for exactly this unexpected quality.

In speaking of pictorial balance, we are almost always referring to horizontal balance, the right and left sides of the image. Artists do consider vertical balance as well, with a horizontal axis dividing top and bottom. Again a certain general equilibrium is usually desirable. However,

because of our sense of gravity, we are readily accustomed to seeing more weight toward the bottom, with the resulting stability and calm **(b)**. The farther up in the format the main distribution of weight or visual interest occurs, the more unstable and dynamic the image becomes. In Paul Klee's whimsical drawing of a *Tightrope Walker* **(c)** this instability of the image expresses the theme perfectly. The linear patterns build up vertically until we reach the teetering figure near the top. The artist can manipulate the vertical balance freely to fit a particular theme or purpose.

a Katsukawa Shunei. *The Actor Nakamura Noshio II.* Before 1819. Woodcut, 12⅞ × 8⅞″ (33 × 23 cm). Private collection.
b Rembrandt. *The Adoration of the Shepherds.* 1640. Oil on canvas, 26 × 21½″ (66 × 55 cm). National Gallery, London (reproduced by courtesy of the Trustees).
c Paul Klee. *Tightrope Walker.* 1923. Color lithograph, 17⅛ × 10⅝″ (44 × 26 cm). Museum of Modern Art, New York (anonymous gift).

a

b

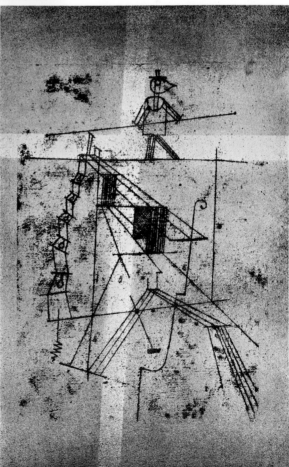

c

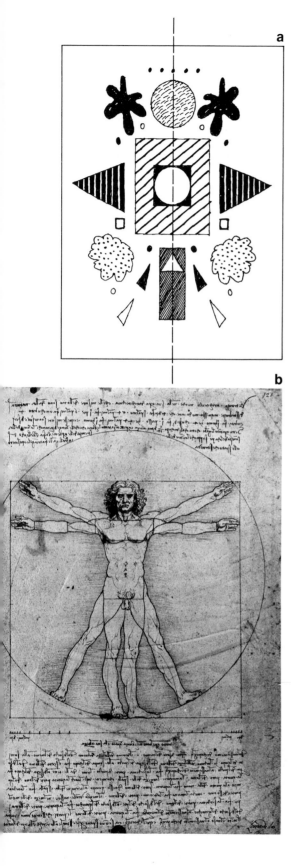

a

b

c

d

Balance

The simplest type of balance—the simplest to create and the simplest to recognize—is called *symmetrical* balance. In symmetrical balance, like shapes are repeated in the same positions on either side of a central vertical axis **(a)**. One side, in effect, becomes the mirror image of the other side. Symmetrical balance has a seemingly basic appeal for us. Children and beginning art students will almost instinctively create patterns with symmetrical balance. Psychologists ascribe this to our awareness of the fact that our bodies are basically symmetrical **(b)**, so that we intuitively extend the principle to our first artistic efforts.

Conscious symmetrical repetition, while clearly creating perfect balance, can be undeniably static, hence the term *formal* balance that is used to describe the same idea. There is nothing wrong with quiet formality. In fact, that is the very characteristic often desired in some art, notably in architecture. The Colonial house **(c)** is a rigidly repetitive pattern, and this results in a dignified, calm, sedate façade—qualities we like in a home. We like a house to look stable, to be a quiet refuge from the world's daily problems. This accounts for the continued popularity, even today, of Colonial-style domestic architecture.

Government buildings, such as state houses, city halls, palaces, and courthouses, often exploit the properties of symmetrical balance. A feeling of enduring permanence and imposing formality is important in such public statements of power. Countless examples are to be found throughout the world.

It should be noted that symmetrical balance does not, by itself, necessarily preordain any specific visual result. Examples **d** and **e** are both symmetrical façades, and yet they create very different impressions. St. Paul's Cathedral **(d)** is a beautifully ordered and dignified image. The Paris Opéra **(e)**, however, is an excitingly ornate "wedding cake," with only the symmetrical organization molding the masses of niches, balustrades, columns, and statuary, into a coherent visual pattern.

a In symmetrical balance, one side of a design mirrors the other.
b Leonardo da Vinci. *Proportions of the Human Figure According to Vitruvius.* c. 1485-90. Pen and ink, 13½ × 9¾″ (34 × 25 cm). Accademia, Venice.
c Vassal (Longfellow) House, Cambridge, Mass. 1750.
d Sir Christopher Wren. West façade, Cathedral of St. Paul, London. 1675-1710.
e Charles Garnier. Façade, The Opéra, Paris. 1861-74.

e

a

b

Balance

Symmetrical balance is rarer in painting than in architecture. However, there are certain instances where it has proved to be a useful compositional device.

Sometimes the subject matter makes symmetrical balance appropriate. A dignified, solemn subject such as the Madonna enthroned **(a)** clearly calls for the qualities symmetrical balance can impart. In this example the Madonna is presented in stately, regal splendor. Her position on the central axis gives her primary emphasis. You will notice that in painting, elements or figures may vary slightly on the opposing sides without changing the basic effect of symmetry. Many religious paintings that were intended as altarpieces in churches employed symmetry so as not to interrupt the prevailing tenor of the architectural setting.

If an artist has a theme involving a great number of figures or elements, then symmetrical balance (which in other cases can be a rather contrived device) can organize the confusion into a logical pattern. Veronese's *Christ in the House of Levi* **(b)** contains a very large number of figures and much activity. The scene could easily be chaotic, but the symmetry provides needed organization. The architecture gives us three clear divisions, and Christ's position on the center axis supplies the focal point.

Contemporary Color Field painting often uses symmetrical balance for a different, very specific reason. This style is sometimes referred to as Minimal Art, since the artists who practice it seek to reduce art to a minimum of aesthetic considerations. Example **c**, a painting by Frank Stella, should explain the concept. To focus our attention on the color relationships, Stella severely plays down all the other elements. Subject matter is ignored, and the repetitive composition of squares lends relatively little visual interest. The symmetrical, formal positioning can be understood quickly and does not intrigue the viewer. Thus, our whole attention is directed to the color. Such paintings make full use of symmetrical balance's one negative aspect—its potential dullness.

a Giovanni Bellini. *Madonna and Child Enthroned (San Giobbe Altarpiece).* c. 1485. Panel, 15′4″ × 8′4″ (4.67 × 2.54 m). Accademia, Venice.
b Paolo Veronese. *Christ in the House of Levi.* 1573. Oil on canvas, 18′2″ × 42′ (5.54 × 12.8 m). Accademia, Venice.
c Frank Stella. *Gran Cairo.* 1962. Synthetic polymer, 7′11½″ (2.17 m) square. Whitney Museum of American Art, New York (gift of Friends of the Whitney Museum of American Art).

c

44

Introduction

The second type of balance is called *asymmetrical* balance. In this case balance is achieved with *dis*similar objects that have equal visual weight or equal eye attraction. Remember the children's riddle: "Which weighs more, a pound of feathers or a pound of lead?" Of course, they both weigh a pound, but the amount and mass of each would vary radically. This is the essence of asymmetrical balance.

In Degas' portrait **(a)** the figure is posed on the left side of the format. On the right side, there is not another figure but a desk littered with papers and books. The light-colored items on the heavy dark shape of the desk provide a complicated visual pattern that attracts the eye. There is enough visual interest here to provide balance for the relatively simple shape of the figure, which draws our primary attention.

The imposing Ford Foundation Building in **b** is an example of asymmetrical balance in architecture. The weight and eye attraction of the

two sides are balanced with very different elements and materials. The strong, simple, rectangular areas of brown granite on the left are visually balanced by the lighter but more intricate window pattern of reflecting glass on the right. This change and contrast provides visual interest and excitement.

In contrast to symmetrical balance, the effect here is more casual, hence the alternate title of *informal* balance that is often used. The effect *is* less formal, less contrived in feeling, and apparently less planned, although obviously this last characteristic is misleading. Asymmetrical balance is actually more intricate and complicated to use than symmetrical balance, which merely repeats elements in a mirror image. More subtle factors are involved in attempting to balance dissimilar items.

a Edgar Degas. *Portrait of Diego Martelli.* 1879. Oil on canvas, 43¼ × 39½" (110 × 100 cm). National Gallery of Scotland, Edinburgh.
b Kevin Roche, John Dinkeloo and Associates, architects. Ford Foundation Building, New York. 1968.

a

b

Balance

Balance by Color

Studies have proved that our eyes are attracted to color. Given a choice, we will always turn our attention to a colored image rather than to one in black and white. Color therefore can become a balancing factor. A small area of bright color, for instance, can balance a much larger area of a duller, more neutral color. Our eyes, drawn by the color, see the smaller element to be as interesting and as "heavy" visually as the larger element.

This technique of achieving balance is common in painting. In the work by Gauguin **(a)** the figure at left is wearing a brilliant red-patterned sarong, the figure at right a muumuu of quite neutral, grayish pink. The areas of color are very different in size, but the artist establishes an equilibrium based on color. Reversing these colors would result in a visual imbalance. The right figure, if dressed in bright, eye-attracting red, would become far too dominant.

In **b** we are outside looking into a *Room in New York,* a painting by Edward Hopper. We do not look at the scene squarely. On the left there is the heavy dark shape of an open window, as well as a glimpse of the pillar outside. The dark piano at right helps to balance this weight, but because the artist painted the girl's dress and the lampshade a brilliant red, our attention is drawn to the right side, and this provides visual balance. The red is not a discordant note; the armchair and painting at left are also red, but of a very subdued, neutral shade.

a Paul Gauguin. *Two Women on a Beach.* 1891.
Oil on canvas, 27 × 35½″ (69 × 90 cm). Louvre, Paris.
b Edward Hopper. *Room in New York.* 1932. Oil on canvas, 29 × 36″ (66 × 91 cm). University of Nebraska Art Galleries, Lincoln (J. M. Hall Collection).

a

b

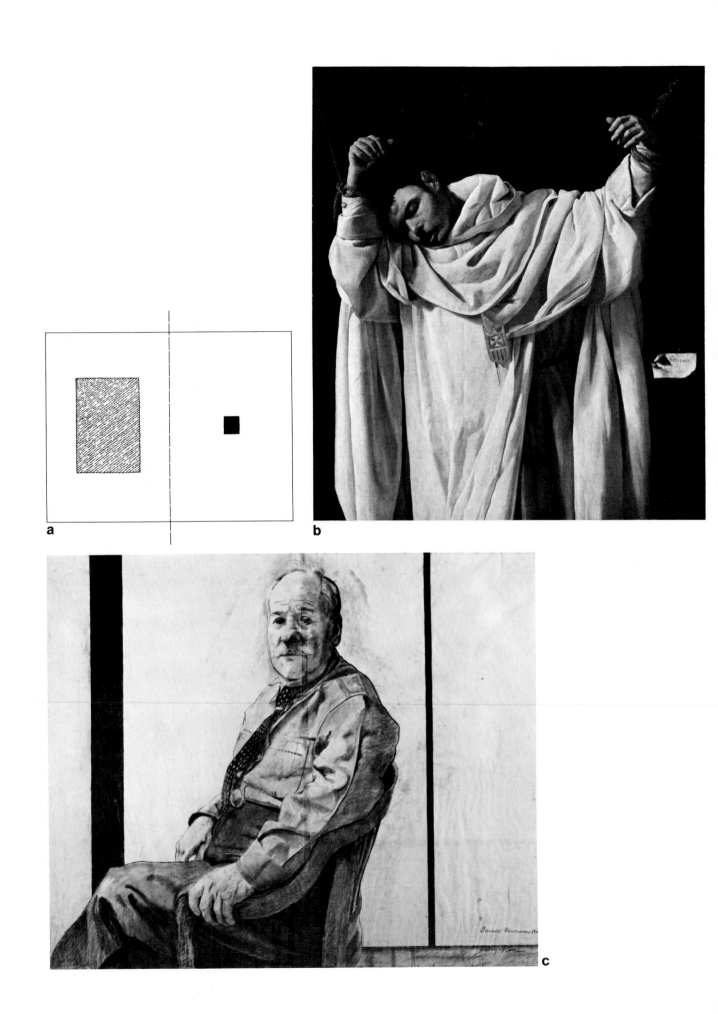

a

b

c

Balance

Balance by Value

Asymmetrical balance is based on equal eye attraction—dissimilar objects that are equally interesting to the eye. One element that attracts our attention is *value* difference, a contrast of light and dark. Example **a** illustrates that black against white is a stronger contrast than gray against white; therefore, a smaller amount of black is needed to visually balance a larger amount of gray.

An application of this idea in an admittedly not-so-subtle manner is Zurbarán's painting **(b)**. The martyred St. Serapion, rather than being centered on the canvas, is mainly on the left side. The saint's head, where our attention naturally goes, is to the left of the center axis. This emphasis is balanced on the right by the greater dark and light contrast in his robes, and also by the piece of paper tacked to the wall—a small white shape contrasting strongly with the very dark background. Without this tiny element, our attention would be focused too strongly on the left side.

Asymmetrical Balance

The drawing by Larry Rivers **(c)** illustrates the same idea. This is a portrait of the artist Barnett Newman, whose paintings often consist of vertical stripes. Rivers cleverly draws upon the stripe theme to balance the image. The head and bulk of the figure is on the center axis, but then a subtle asymmetry is achieved. The pose carries the eye to the left, where the artist has placed the hands and noticeably the legs overlapping a stripe. The right side is balanced by the narrow but dark vertical stripe that attracts our attention for its value contrast with the light background.

In **d** a small glimpse of bright sky contributes to the painting's balance.

a A darker, smaller element is visually equal to a lighter, larger one.
b Francisco de Zurbarán. *St. Serapion.* 1628. Oil on canvas, 47½ × 40¾″ (121 × 104 cm). Wadsworth Atheneum, Hartford, Conn. (Ella Gallup Sumner and Mary Catlin Sumner Collection).
c Larry Rivers. Working drawing for *The Stripe is in the Eye of the Beholder.* 1975. Pencil, 7′1¾″ × 8′4½″ (2.18 × 2.55 m). Collection David Pincus, Wynnewood, Pa.
d Anne-Louis Girodet-Trioson. *The Entombment of Atala.* 1808. Oil on canvas, 6′11¾″ × 8′9″ (2.13 × 2.67 m). Louvre, Paris.

d

Balance

Balance by Shape

The diagram in **a** illustrates balance by shape. Here the two elements are exactly the same color, exactly the same value and texture. The only difference is their shape. The smaller form attracts the eye because of its more complicated contours. Though small, it is equally as interesting as the much larger, but duller, rectangle.

This type of balance appears in Goya's painting *The Parasol* **(b)**. The standing figure is on the central axis, with the lady seated slightly to the left. On the left also is the quite large shape of the parasol defined against a simple dark area of shadowed wall. Clearly, something is needed on the right for balance, and Goya chose the tree that leans to the right. This tree, while slender and delicate, has an intricate pattern of branches and leaves to balance the very simple, elliptical shape of the parasol. In the back-

ground, the small shapes of tree foliage are easily as interesting as the large, dark, somewhat geometric, triangular shadow at left. To put it briefly: the left side consists of large simple shapes, the right side of smaller, more complicated areas. Together they achieve balance.

The balance of elements in the Japanese print **(c)** resembles that in the Goya painting. Here the large, simple shape of the girl is left of the center axis. The tree branch with many small blossom shapes creates an intricate pattern that gives balance on the right side.

a A small, complicated shape is balanced by a larger, more stable shape.
b Francisco Goya. Cartoon for tapestry, *The Parasol.* 1777. Oil on canvas, approx. 3′5″ × 4′11″ (1.04 × 1.5 m). Prado, Madrid.
c Suzuki Harunobu. *Girl with Lantern on a Balcony at Night.* c. 1768. Color woodcut, 12¾ × 8¼″ (32 × 21 cm). Metropolitan Museum of Art, New York (Fletcher Fund, 1929).

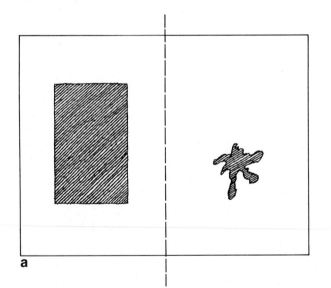

a

b

c

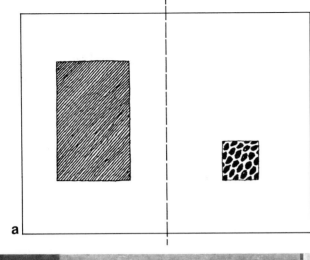

a

b

c

d

Balance

Balance by Texture

Any visual (or photographic) texture having a variegated dark and light pattern holds more interest for the eye than a smooth, unrelieved surface. The drawing in **a** presents this idea: the smaller, rough-textured area balances the larger, basically untextured area (smoothness is, in a sense, a "texture").

The subject of Vermeer's *Lady With a Lute* **(b)** sits slightly to the left of the center axis and *looks* to the left, further emphasizing that side of the painting. The major balancing element on the right is, of course, the large map on the wall. Important to this composition is the rather busy, detailed texture of light and dark variations; a plain, flat brown area would not have brought the necessary interest. The shiny nail heads on the dark chair contribute a further balancing interest.

Whistler's mother (actually entitled *Arrangement in Grey and Black, No. 1*) is such a familiar image that we often do not give it more than a glance **(c)**. Actually, it is quite a subtle painting if we can look beyond the Mother's Day sentimentality. The almost silhouetted lady is on the right, her dark shape offset by a careful arrangement of the several neutral-colored rectangles at left. The light picture with the dark linear frame draws the eye, as does the large, dark area of the curtain. But notice how important is the delicate suggestion of gray-and-white pattern on this drapery. The pattern adds much visual interest to that area and is vital to the picture's balance.

The shiny, reflective surfaces of a silver tea set are the major element in balancing the figures in a painting by Mary Cassatt **(d)**.

Printed text consisting of letters and words in effect creates a visual texture. This is information in symbols that we can read, but the *visual* effect is nothing more than a gray patterned shape. Depending on the typeface and the layout, this gray area varies in darkness, density, and character, but it is visually textured nevertheless. The Olivetti advertisement in **e** illustrates this point. Here the small paragraph of text creates a textured area that visually balances the larger shape of the sickle.

a A small, textured shape can balance a larger, untextured one.
b Jan Vermeer. *Lady with a Lute.* 1663-64. Oil on canvas, 20¼ × 18″ (51 × 46 cm). Metropolitan Museum of Art, New York (bequest of Collis P. Huntington, 1925).
c James Abbott McNeill Whistler. *Arrangement in Grey and Black No. 1, The Artist's Mother.* 1871. Oil on canvas, 4′9″ × 5′4½″ (1.45 × 1.64 m). Louvre, Paris.
d Mary Cassatt. *A Cup of Tea.* c. 1880. Oil on canvas, 25½ × 36½″ (65 × 83 cm). Museum of Fine Arts, Boston (Maria Hopkins Fund).
e Two-page layout from *Early American Tools* (Olivetti Corporation of America). Irwin Glusker, art director and designer; Hans Namuth, photographer.

e

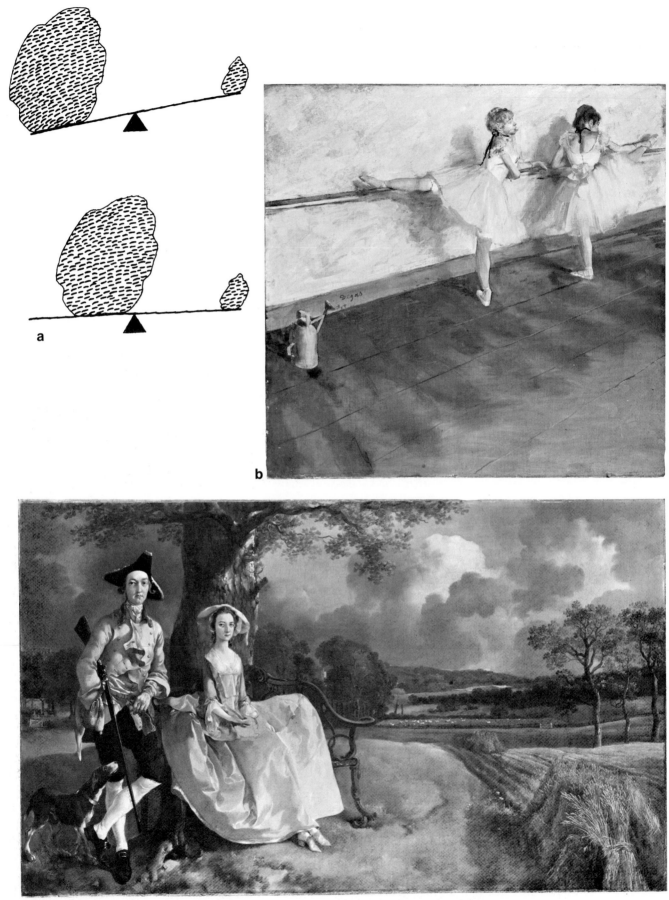

a

b

c

Balance

Balance by Position

The two see-saw diagrams in **a** illustrate the idea of balance by position. It is a well-known principle in physics that two items of unequal weight can be brought to equilibrium by moving the heavier inward toward the fulcrum. In design this means that a large item placed closer to the center can be balanced by a smaller item placed out toward the edge.

Balance by position often lends an unusual, unexpected quality to the composition. The effect not only seems casual and unplanned, but it can indeed, at first glance, seem to be imbalance. A painting by Degas **(b)** shows this quality. With the two dancers mainly to the right of center, the only balancing element on the left is the small gray watering can. However, its placement, isolated at the left edge of the painting, can visually balance the much larger figures.

An unusual painting by Gainsborough **(c)** has obvious emphasis on the left, where the two figures are posed before a large tree. The three detailed trees and the wheat sheaves are smaller elements, but their placement at far right, running off the edge of the picture, provides a very subtle balance.

Bacchus and Ariadne by Titian **(d)** presents the same idea in a slightly less obvious way. The trees and the vast number of figures on the right move our eyes to the center, where the figure of Bacchus is almost on the center axis. Principles of color and value contrast also contribute to balancing the left side, but the main factor is the position of Ariadne's figure on the edge of the format. Mentally move this figure toward the center, and you can imagine the imbalance that results.

a A large shape placed near the middle of a design can be balanced by a smaller shape placed toward the outer edge.
b Edgar Degas. *Dancers Practicing at the Barre.* 1877. Oil on canvas, 29¾ × 32″ (76 × 81 cm). Metropolitan Museum of Art, New York (H. O. Havemeyer Collection).
c Thomas Gainsborough. *Mr. and Mrs. Robert Andrews.* c. 1748–50. Oil on canvas, 27 × 47″ (69 × 119 cm). National Gallery, London (reproduced by courtesy of the Trustees).
d Titian. *Bacchus and Ariadne.* c. 1520. Oil on canvas, 5′8″ × 6⅞″ (1.73 × 1.85 m). National Gallery, London (reproduced by courtesy of the Trustees).

d

Balance

Balance by Eye Direction

One further element in achieving asymmetrical balance should be noted. In **a** the many heavier elements on the right all direct our attention automatically to the left, thus building up the smallest of elements into a balancing importance. Asymmetrical balance is based on equal eye attraction, and here the large elements themselves make the small element a focal emphasis.

In Seurat's painting **(b)** the small, white gaslight form at left assumes great visual importance from the number of elements that lead our eyes to that side. All the dancers face and kick their legs in this direction, and the dark, diagonal, linear shape of the bass fiddle takes the eye right to this light shape. Almost everywhere we look something works to move our eyes back to that one seemingly unimportant element that balances the whole picture.

In this method of balance, the direction in which figures look also applies, because we

viewers will involuntarily look the same way. Figures **c** and **d** illustrate this idea. The soldier's backward glance in Géricault's painting **(c)** helps to balance the leftward movement and the interest of the horse's head and prancing leg at the left side of the painting. In Eakins' portrait of *Miss Van Buren* **(d)** the leaning of the figure to the right and the head (the focal point) on the right side are balanced by the subject's definite gaze to the left, a gaze that we follow.

While not usually the *only* technique of balance employed, this useful device of eye direction is a common practice among artists.

a A single small element can be as important as many larger ones if it is made the focal point of the design.
b Georges Seurat. *Le Chahut.* 1890. Oil on canvas, 5'7" × 4'7" (1.69 × 1.39 m). Rijksmuseum Kröller-Müller, Otterlo, Netherlands.
c Théodore Géricault. *Wounded Cuirassier Leaving the Field.* 1814. Oil on canvas, c. 9'7" × 7'5⅜" (2.95 × 2.27 m). Louvre, Paris.
d Thomas Eakins. *Miss Van Buren.* 1889–91. Oil on canvas, 45 × 32" (110 × 81 cm). Phillips Collection, Washington, D.C.

a

b

d

c

a

b

Balance

Analysis Summary

In looking at paintings, you will realize that isolating one technique of asymmetrical balance as we have done is a bit misleading, since the vast majority of works employ several of the methods simultaneously. For the sake of clarity these methods are discussed separately, but the principles often overlap and are often used together. Let us look at just two examples that make use of several of the factors involved in asymmetrical balance.

In *The Mill near Wijk* **(a)** Ruisdael placed a large windmill to the right of the center axis. Elements must be organized on the left to counterbalance this very obvious focal point. First, the sky at left has some large, dark clouds that provide more value contrast than the sky on the other side. The small boat is also highlighted by value—the white sail against dark sky and the dark hull on the shimmering white water. The boat's position close to the edge also contributes to the balance, since the mill is located nearer the axis. But, most importantly, the tiny boat is emphasized by a large, dark land mass that narrows and makes, in effect, a triangular arrow pointing our eyes at the boat. Incidentally, the opposing arrow of the water leading to the lower right has no definite conclusion. Pilings and weeds conveniently obscure the actual point, so the eye is not led out of the picture entirely.

The multiple portrait of *The Daughters of Edward Darley Boit* **(b)** by Sargent has an interesting composition with fairly isolated figures and a great amount of dark negative space. The initial emphasis is at the left, where the large vase and almost all the figures are posed. Only the little girl seated on the rug is very slightly to the right of center. The right side of the composition is basically empty space, but a few visually important elements balance the painting. A window in the rear room provides two light areas in high contrast with the darkness. The glimpse of red curtain at right introduces the brightest color note in the whole painting. And, finally, the light shape of the second large vase draws our eyes to the very edge of the painting, offsetting the figures clustered near the center.

Most paintings would exhibit this same combination of balancing devices.

a Jacob van Ruisdael. *The Mill near Wijk.* c. 1670. Oil on canvas, 33 × 40″ (84 × 102 cm). Rijksmuseum, Amsterdam.
b John Singer Sargent. *The Daughters of Edward Darley Boit.* 1882. Oil on canvas, 7′3⅝″ (2.23 m) square. Museum of Fine Arts, Boston (gift of the daughters of Edward Darley Boit in memory of their father).

Balance

Radial Balance

A third variety of balance is called *radial* balance. Here all the elements radiate or circle out from a common central point. The sun with its emanating rays **(a)** is a familiar symbol that expresses the basic idea. Radial balance is not entirely distinct from symmetrical or asymmetrical balance. It is merely a refinement of one or the other, depending on whether the focus occurs in the middle or off-center.

Circular forms abound in certain craft areas such as ceramics, where the round shapes of dishes and bowls often make radial balance a natural choice in decorating such objects. Radial balance also appears in jewelry design. The brooch in **b** is reminiscent of the radial patterns found in snowflakes. Notice how each of the small outer elements makes a radial design in itself. Radial balance has been used frequently in architecture. The round form of domed buildings such as the Roman Pantheon **(c)** will almost automatically lend a radial feeling to the interior.

The major compositional advantage in radial balance is the immediate and obvious creation of a focal point. Perhaps, in a way, this is the very reason such balance seldom occurs in painting. It might seem a little too contrived and unnatural, a little *too* obvious to be entirely satisfactory. There can be no doubt that when radial balance *is* used in painting, it is

employed in a rather understated manner. Utrillo's Parisian street scene **(d)** has a quite clear radial feeling. The one-point perspective of the receding curbs and rooflines directs the eye to the white cathedral in the distance.

Less obvious, but still with a definite radial feeling, is Bouts' *Last Supper* **(e)**. The positioning of the disciples around the table, all turned and looking inward, creates the radial effect. We can see that the plate in the center of the table is truly more of a focal point than the figure of Christ, which becomes another of the radiating elements.

The fact that radial balance is rare in formal, narrative painting should not deter you from experimenting with it. It can be a useful tool in organization, and some extremely effective designs may result.

a Jean Lurçat. *Soleil-Sagittaire*, 1960. Tapestry, 7'1⅛" × 9'11" (2.2 × 3.05 m). Courtesy Madame Lurçat.
b Helga and Bent Exner. Brooch in white gold and tugtupite, created for H.R.H. Queen Ingrid of Denmark, c. 1972.
c Giovanni Paolo Pannini. *The Interior of the Pantheon.* c. 1750. Oil on canvas, 4'2½" × 3'3" (1.28 × .99 m). National Gallery of Art, Washington, D.C. (Samuel H. Kress Collection, 1939).
d Maurice Utrillo. *Church of Le Sacre Coeur, Montmartre et Rue Saint-Rustique.* Oil on canvas, 19½ × 24" (50 × 61 cm). Museum of Fine Arts, Boston (bequest of John T. Spalding).
e Dirk Bouts. *Last Supper Altarpiece*, detail. 1464–67. Panel c. 6' × 5'⅛" (1.83 × 1.53 m). Church of St.-Pierre, Louvain.

a

b

c

d

e

Balance

Allover Pattern

One more specific type of visual effect is often designated as a fourth variety of balance. The examples here illustrate the idea. These works all exhibit an equal emphasis over the whole format—the same weight or eye attraction literally everywhere. This is officially called *crystallographic balance.* Since few people can remember this term, and even fewer can spell it, the more common name is *allover pattern.* This is, of course, a rather special refinement of symmetrical balance. But the constant repetition of the same quality everywhere on the surface *is* truly a different impression from our usual concept of symmetrical balance.

Pollock's nonobjective, expressionist painting *Autumn Rhythm* **(a)** has no focal point, no beginning and no end, but rather a terribly complicated pattern that extends without real change over the whole canvas.

In **b** Mondrian's *Broadway Boogie-Woogie* perhaps has a focal point of sorts in the larger area at upper right center. However, the overall impression is a jumpy, staccato pattern of small squares repeating the primary colors of red, yellow, and blue.

Fabric patterns, with their purposeful lack of any focal point, are usually distinguished by a constant repetition of the same motif **(c)**.

Vasarely's serigraph **(d)** has a repetitive pattern of almost identical elements over the whole surface. This uniformity of emphasis focuses our attention on the color and value relationships. The usual concept of balancing elements does not apply when *every* element is equally stressed in visual importance.

a Jackson Pollock. *Autumn Rhythm.* 1950. Oil on canvas, 8'9" × 17'3" (2.59 × 5.26 m). Metropolitan Museum of Art, New York (George A. Hearn Fund, 1957).
b Piet Mondrian. *Broadway Boogie-Woogie.* 1942–43. Oil on canvas, 4'2" (1.27 m) square. Museum of Modern Art, New York (anonymous gift).
c In some instances, as in fabric patterns, a focal point is deliberately excluded.
d Victor Vasarely. *Untitled,* from the series *CTA 102.* 1966. Serigraph, 35¼" (90 cm) square. Museum of Modern Art, New York (purchase).

a

b

c

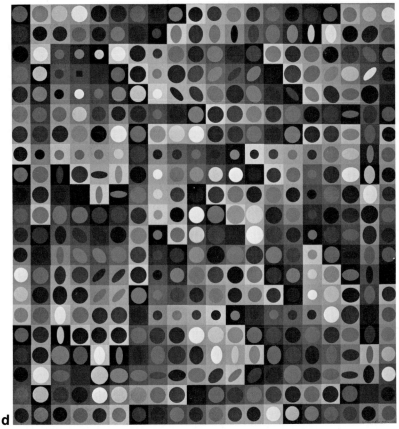

d

Scale / Proportion

Scale/Proportion Introduction

Scale and proportion are similar terms with a slightly different emphasis. *Scale* refers essentially to size; "large scale" is a way of saying big, and "small scale" just means small. "Big" and "small," however, are relative. What is big? Big is meaningless unless we have some standard of reference. A *big* dog means nothing if we do not know the size of most dogs. This is what separates the two terms. *Proportion* refers to *relative* size, size measured against other elements or against some mental norm or standard. Look at the design in **a**. Here the large black circle would certainly be called large scale. It is a large element and occupies much space, given the overall dimensions of the design. It could also be described as *out of proportion*. Compared to the other tiny elements, it is *too* large and overwhelms the rest of the pattern, demanding all our visual attention. The

phrase *out of scale* could also be applied to that big circle, implying the same fault.

Scale and proportion are closely tied to emphasis and focal point. Large scale and especially large size in proportion to other elements makes for an obvious visual emphasis. In **b** the eye goes naturally first to the large-scale figure in the center. The artist Honoré Sharrer has created a focal point that dominates the other small figures in the windows of the building in the background.

a The large circle, out of proportion to the other elements, overwhelms them.
b Honoré Sharrer. *The Industrial Scene*, center panel of *Tribute to the American Working People*. 1945–50. Oil on canvas. Courtesy Knoedler Gallery, New York.

a

b

a

b

c

Scale/Proportion

There are two ways to think of artistic scale. One is to consider the scale of the work itself, its size in relation to other art, in relation to its surroundings, or in relation to human size. Unhappily, the one thing book illustrations cannot do is show art in its original size or scale. Unusual or unexpected scale is arresting and attention-getting. Sheer size *does* impress us.

When we are confronted by frescoes such as the Sistine Chapel ceiling, our first reaction is simply awe at the enormous scope of the work. Later, we study and admire details, but first we are overwhelmed by the sheer magnitude. The reverse effect is illustrated in **a**. It comes as a shock to stand before this actual painting, for it is tiny, 5 by 5¾ inches—barely larger than what you see opposite. The exquisite detail, the delicate precision of the drawing, and the color subtleties all impress us. Our first thought has to be of the fantastic difficulty of achieving such effects in so tiny a format.

If large or small size springs naturally from the function, theme, or purpose of a work, obvi-

ously an unusual scale is justified. We are acquainted with many such cases. The gigantic pyramids made a political statement of the Pharaohs' eternal power. The elegant miniatures of the religious Book of Hours **(b)** served as book illustrations for the private devotionals of a medieval nobility. The small detailed golden saltcellar **(c)** graced a regal dining table. Even the scale of Oldenburg's 9-foot-high *Falling Shoestring Potatoes* **(d)** has a purpose—that of ridiculing the importance that is accorded the banal aspects of life in Western civilization.

a Follower of Jan van Eyck. *St. Francis Receiving the Stigmata.* Early 15th century. Oil on panel, 5 × 5¾″ (13 × 15 cm). Galleria Sabauda, Turin.
b Limbourg Brothers. *Multiplication of the Loaves and Fishes,* from the Book of Hours (Les Très Riches Heures) of the Duke of Berry. 1416. Illumination, 6¼ × 4⅜″ (16 × 11 cm). Musée Condé, Chantilly.
c Benvenuto Cellini. *Saltcellar of Francis I.* 1539–43. Gold, 10¼ × 13″ (26 × 33 cm). Kunsthistorisches Museum, Vienna.
d Claes Oldenburg. *Falling Shoestring Potatoes.* 1965. Painted canvas, kapok; height 9′ (2.74 m). Walker Art Center, Minneapolis (gift of the T. B. Walker Foundation).

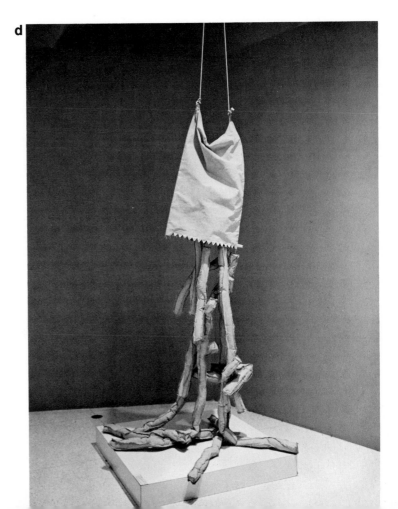

Scale/Proportion

When the artist Christo constructed *Running Fence* **(a)** in northern California, it was a very controversial project. Admittedly, the idea of a nylon fence running through some 24 miles of rolling suburban hills to the ocean is unique as an artistic expression. Such an environmental project, forcing us to see the familiar world around us in a special way, does not fit some people's definition of art. However, even those skeptical of the fence's aesthetic contribution had to be impressed by the sheer scale of such a work. It is undoubtedly true that *Running Fence* was most impressive from an aerial view, where the enormous scale could be realized in the context of its setting.

Probably no motif from contemporary art has been reproduced so many times for so many different purposes as Robert Indiana's *Love* **(b)**. It has been the decorative theme of T-shirts, coffee mugs, matchbook covers, wall posters, bracelet charms, postage stamps, cocktail napkins, and myriad other things. Each time, in each medium, it has changed scale; but each time it remained graphically appealing to a large audience. This would seem to be proof of the image's absolute brilliance or utter fatuousness—that it could be effective in so many different sizes and contexts.

Unusual scale in a work of art should have a thematic or functional justification. Bigness for the sake of bigness, simply to gain attention, is usually a mistake. The illustrative anecdotes of 19th-century salon art were often enormous in scale, but this simply made the emptiness and pretentiousness all the more painfully obvious. Example **c** is a sentimental, trivial scene. Did it truly *need* to be almost 5 feet by 4 feet in size? Be sure you know in your mind *why* your design should be overlarge or very tiny.

a Christo. *Running Fence.* 1972–76. Nylon fabric and steel poles, 18′ × 24½ miles. Installed in Sonoma and Marin counties, California, 1976, for two weeks.
b Robert Indiana. *Love.* 1966. Carved aluminum, 12 × 12 × 6″ (30 × 30 × 15 cm). Courtesy Multiples, Inc., New York.
c Adolphe Bouguereau. *The Thank Offering.* 1867. Oil on canvas, 4′10″ × 3′6¼″ (1.47 × 1.07 m). Philadelphia Museum of Art (Wilstach Collection, given by John G. Johnson).

a

b

c

Scale/Proportion

The second way to discuss artistic scale is to consider the size and scale of elements *within* the design or pattern. The scale here, of course, is relative to the overall area of the format; a big element in one painting might be considered small in a larger work.

The three examples in **a** show how variations in scale can yield very different design effects. Having elements of differing sizes brings visual interest and, as you can see, affects the emphasis. Which design is "best" or which we prefer can be argued. The answer would depend upon what effect we wish to create.

Look at the difference scale can make in a painting. Examples **b** and **c** both have the same theme, the Crucifixion of Christ. In Tintoretto's painting **(b)** tiny figures crowd the scene, and Christ is small scale, barely identifiable. Tintoretto gives us a vast panorama of events. We see the thieves crucified with Christ, the soldiers gambling for His robe, the mob, all the various facets of the story. In contrast, the El Greco painting puts Christ in very large scale **(c)**. We concentrate in this work on the personal agony of Christ. The rest of the story is forgotten or ignored. Both the paintings are emotional images, but the scale of the elements results in contrasting impressions.

a Changes in scale within a design also change the total effect.
b Jacopo Tintoretto. *The Crucifixion.* 1565. Oil on canvas, 17′7″ × 40′2″ (5.36 × 12.24 m). Sala dell'Albergo, Scuola di San Rocco, Venice.
c El Greco. *Christ on the Cross with Landscape.* c. 1600–10. Oil on canvas, 6′2″ × 3′8″ (1.88 × 1.12 m). Cleveland Museum of Art (gift of Hanna Fund).

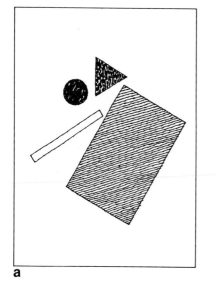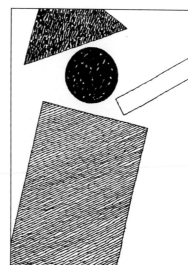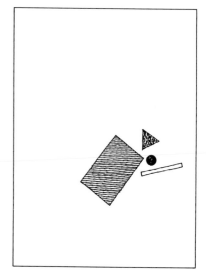

a

b

c

a

b

Actual Size!

This time last year, you compared fists, feet, hands with those of real jocks,
Ali, Foreman, Lanier, Walton. You were so humiliated, you deserve another
shot. Here it is, by popular demand, your rematch. Pit your parts against
the pros', from body builder to lady jockey, from neck bone to thigh bone.

Arnold Schwarzenegger's biceps

Photographed by George Butler

Scale/Proportion

We have seen how scale can attract our attention in different ways, depending on the artist's purpose. Scale can also be used to draw our notice to the unexpected or exaggerated, as when small objects are magnified or large ones reduced. An unusually large close-up, such as Mark Fennessey's drawing **(a)**, makes a small insect into a quite terrifying, powerful image. The scale of the drawing therefore is essential to its effect.

In magazines, editorial pages and advertisements compete for the casual reader's attention. The almost page-filling image of a body-builder's muscular biceps **(b)** gets this attention by the unusually large scale within the format.

A men's clothing store took the opposite approach for an advertising campaign **(c)**. A small, elegantly clad figure is isolated in a vast, empty space emphasized by the city skyline far in the distance. Again, the unexpected scale provides visual interest.

a Mark Fennessey. *Insect.* 1965–66. Wash drawing. Yale University Art Gallery, New Haven, Conn.
b Two-page spread from *Esquire,* October 1975, showing Arnold Schwarzenegger's biceps. Art director, Richard Weigand; photographer, George Butler. © 1975 Esquire, Inc.
c Advertisement for Wilkes Bashford, San Francisco. Design, Walter Sparks and David Gauger; photograph, Peter Ogilvie; copy, Larry Silva; agency, Gauger, Sparks, Silva.

The detail of Dimitri. Available only at San Francisco's ultimate men's store.

Wilkes Bashford

336 Sutter, San Francisco (415)986-4380

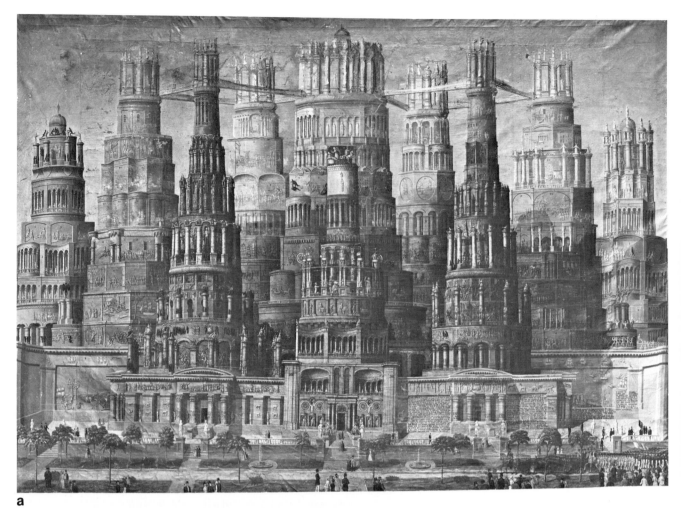

a

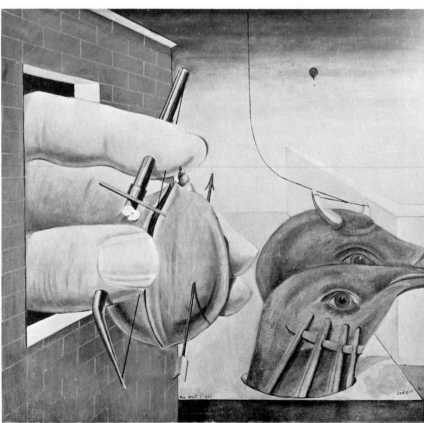

b

Scale/Proportion

The deliberate changing of natural scale is not unusual in painting. In religious paintings many artists have arbitrarily increased the size of the Christ or Virgin figure to emphasize philosophic and religious importance.

Some artists, however, use scale changes intentionally to intrigue or mystify us, rather than to clarify the focal point. Figure **a** is an unusual painting by the American artist Erastus Field. In viewing it, we are struck immediately by the image of this impossibly enormous building. The many tall towers, the almost countless colonnades, the statuary all in a veritable maze of architectural details combine to create a truly incredible building. Some tiny figures and some trees in the foreground set the gigantic scale. The artist has painted a vision, an image totally outside our experience.

Surrealism is an art form based on paradox, on images that simply cannot be explained in rational terms. Artists who work in this manner present the irrational world of the dream or nightmare—recognizable elements in impossible situations. The painting by Ernst **(b)** shows one such enigma, with much of the mystery stemming from a confusion of scale. We identify the various elements easily enough, but they are all the "wrong" size and strange in proportion to each other. For example, we just do not know how to interpret that large hand coming out the window. Are we seeing the hand of a giant or the window of a doll's house? Neither explanation makes any sense.

How can we rationally explain **c**? Another Surrealist artist, René Magritte, has so altered the normal scale relationships we encounter in life that, in a very simple picture, he creates an intriguing puzzle.

a Erastus Salisbury Field. *Historical Monument of the American Republic.* c. 1876. Oil on canvas, 9′3″ × 13′1″ (2.82 × 3.99 m). Museum of Fine Arts, Springfield, Mass. (Morgan Wesson Memorial Collection).
b Max Ernst. *Oedipus Rex.* 1922. Oil on canvas, 35 × 45¾″ (89 × 116 cm). Private collection, Paris.
c René Magritte. *The Listening Chamber.* 1953. Oil on canvas, 31¼ × 39″ (80 × 100 cm). Collection William N. Copley, New York.

c

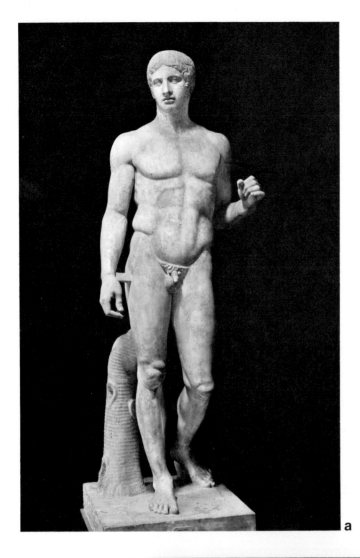

a

b

Scale/Proportion

Most often when we hear the phrase "out of proportion," it relates to pictures of the human body. This expression seems to accompany all our first efforts at life drawing. In this situation we are attempting a picture of the model before us, and the proportions should duplicate those of the figure we see. Faults in proportion (head too small, leg too long, arm too thin, and so forth) become evident right away. But we apply the term also to drawings or paintings in which we have no idea at all of the figures (if any) who modeled. Apparently, we have some abstract mental concept of what is right and what is wrong in the proportions of the human body.

It may be hard to believe, but many of our ideas about human proportions were set almost 2500 years ago. The idealism that marked the Classical Age of Greek art extended to a search for the ideal body proportions. No human figure was considered perfect; it was the role of the artist to create the perfection not found in nature. Actual rules or *canons* of proportion were established. "Correct" proportions were defined by using a part of the body as a unit measurement. For example, the ideal body was determined to be so many heads high. The

sculpture in **a** shows one of the countless examples produced using these almost mathematical formulas. So important was this phase of Greek art that it has exerted a continuing, recurrent influence on generations of artists for hundreds of years.

To speak of ideal proportions in the human body is difficult, because societies change their minds periodically about what constitutes human beauty. Examples **b** and **c** show just one contrast. Both paintings depict Athena, Hera, and Aphrodite, goddesses who epitomized not only grace but perfect beauty and elegance. The two sets of bodies certainly differ in proportions, and undoubtedly neither image would fit our current ideas of feminine beauty. Even today there are dramatic proportional differences between the high-fashion model and the popular entertainment heroine.

a Polyclitus. *Spear Carrier*. Roman copy of Greek original of c. 450-440 B.C. Marble, height 6'6" (1.98 m). National Museum, Naples.
b Peter Paul Rubens. *The Judgment of Paris*, detail. c. 1638. Panel, 4'9½" × 6'4⅜" (1.45 × 1.79 m). National Gallery, London (reproduced by courtesy of the Trustees).
c Lucas Cranach the Elder. *The Judgment of Paris*, detail. 1530. Panel, 13¾ × 9½" (35 × 24 cm). Staatliche Kunsthalle, Karlsruhe.

c

Scale/Proportion

Many artists of many periods have rejected the classical Greek proportions for the human body—even the Greeks themselves as time passed. In contrast to the Greek taste for depicting nudes, medieval figures were clothed and, in fact, often denied the sense of any body underneath the drapery. The natural world of the flesh was rejected to emphasize the inner world of the religious spirit. The Saint Matthew in **a** is an angular, highly abstracted form with very unnatural proportions. This strangely twisted, elongated body, with its very small head, almost completely ignores human proportions and natural anatomy.

Most often body proportions are purposely distorted for the sake of expression, to present an emotional image. Even if we knew nothing of the Roman empress Messalina, we could discern a great deal of her character from Beardsley's drawing in **b**. The ominous, pervading black focuses our attention on Messalina's tiny,

crabbed face, her enlarged, bare, lustful breasts, and the huge, pompous, feathered headdress. This is an obvious image of evil.

Distorted body proportions in Picasso's painting *The Old Guitarist* **(c)** stress the debilitation of old age. The melancholy droop of the head leads the viewer's eye to the elongated thin arms and legs, which create sharp, angular patterns. Both hands and feet, being enlarged bony distortions, become expressive forms. Thus, the proportions, along with the color, create a truly pathetic figure.

a *Saint Matthew,* miniature from the Four Gospels. English, c. 1040. Pierpont Morgan Library, New York.
b Aubrey Beardsley. *Messalina Returning Home.* 1895. Illustration for the sixth satire of Juvenal. Pencil, India ink, and watercolor; 11 × 7″ (28 × 18 cm). Tate Gallery, London.
c Pablo Picasso. *The Old Guitarist.* 1903. Oil on panel, 47¾ × 32½″ (121 × 83 cm). Art Institute of Chicago (Helen Birch Bartlett Memorial Collection).

a

b

c

Scale/Proportion

The Golden Mean

Take a straight line and divide it into two parts so as to create the "perfect" visual relationship of one part to the other. Or, pick the "perfect" rectangle from those shown in **a**—the one having the ideal visual proportion of length to width. Maybe these sound like impossible tasks, or even silly ones, but many artists of the past have concerned themselves with just such problems. The creation of perfect proportions for purely abstract shapes has fascinated many people, part of the fascination being that there is no definite answer. In dividing the line into two parts, we may conclude safely that a division right in the middle would *not* be the most interesting solution. But from there on, the question is literally wide open.

Why do this? Why bother with such an abstract, theoretical problem? If an answer could be agreed upon, then those proportions or size relationships could be applied to actual works of art. The ancient Greeks felt that they had indeed solved this question of perfect proportions. In constructing a rectangle, this concept stated the following ratio: width is to length as length is to width plus length (algebraically, $a:b = b:[a + b]$). This ideal relationship was called the *Golden Mean* (or *Golden Section*). To divide a line in this manner is a geometrical exercise that does not really concern us at this point. We could argue, of course, that any such "rule" is too rigid. Still, the formula has en-

dured for a surprising length of time and has appeared recurrently in art. It was used in designing Greek temples, such as the Parthenon **(b)**, which is probably the most universally admired building ever constructed in Western art.

While most artists today would reject any such rule, certain classical artists of the past have been guided by a form of the Golden Mean in composing their paintings. The painting is arranged by a regular formula. Example **c**, a work by the French artist Claude Lorrain, is analyzed in **d**. A diagonal is drawn from one corner to another. From that diagonal a 90-degree vertical is drawn to one of the other corners. Claude placed the focal point where these lines intersect and used a horizontal and vertical from this point to organize the rest of the painting. This location for the focal point is visually satisfactory. However, few artists or critics today would agree that it is the *best* or only ideal arrangement.

a Different people would pick different rectangles as having "perfect proportions."

b Ictinus and Callicrates. The Parthenon, view from the west. 448–432 B.C. Acropolis, Athens.

c Claude Lorrain. *A Seaport.* 1644. Oil on canvas, 3'3″ × 4'3″ (.99 × 1.3 m). National Gallery, London (reproduced by courtesy of the Trustees).

d An analysis of *A Seaport* **(c)** demonstrates an application of the Golden Mean.

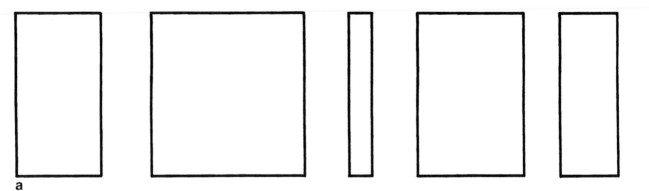

a

Illusion of Space

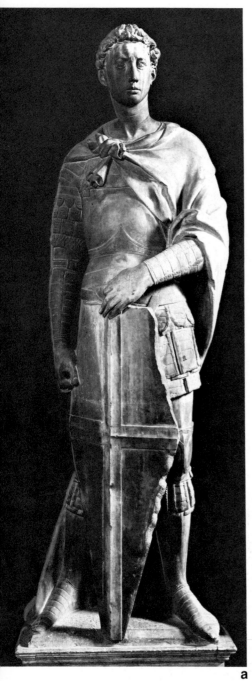

a

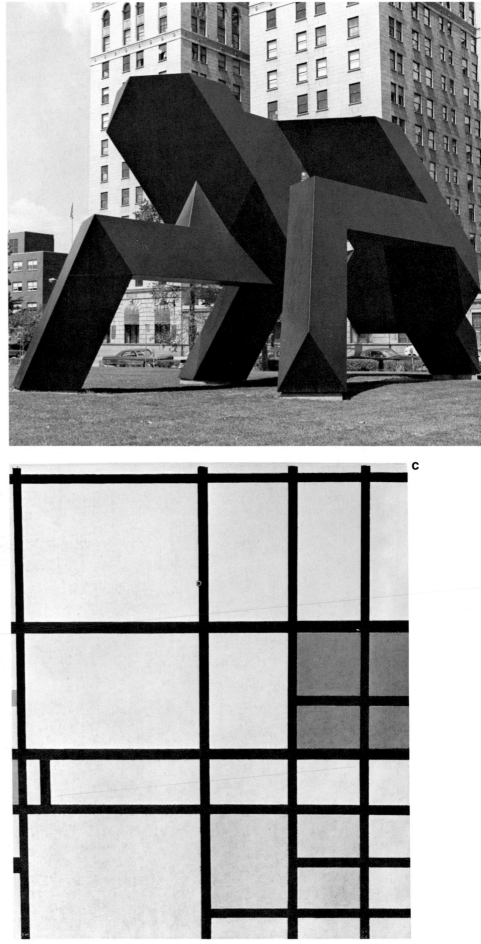

b

c

Illusion of Space

Several art forms are three-dimensional and therefore occupy space: ceramics, jewelry and metalwork, weaving, and sculpture, to name a few. In traditional sculpture like Donatello's **(a)** or in a purely abstract pattern of forms such as Tony Smith's work **(b)**, it is important for us to move about and enjoy the changing spatial patterns from various angles. Architecture, of course, is an art form whose main preoccupation is the enclosure of three-dimensional space.

In two-dimensional art forms, such as drawing, painting, and prints, the artist often desires to give us a feeling of space or depth. Here space is merely an illusion, for the images rendered on paper, canvas, or board are essentially flat.

This illusion of space is the option of the artist. Mondrian in his painting **(c)** does nothing to encourage us to see "back" into his composition. There is no suggestion of depth. The composition is a flat pattern that remains on the *picture plane*—the frontal plane of the canvas. On the other hand, Ruisdael, in his landscape **(d)**, pierces the picture plane, asking us to forget that the painting is a flat piece of canvas and giving us an illusion of great depth, an image full of air and space. The picture plane no longer exists as a plane but becomes a "window" into a simulated three-dimensional world created by the artist.

Through the centuries, artists have studied this problem of presenting an illusion of space, and several devices have been developed.

a Donatello. *St. George.* c. 1417. Marble, height 6′8¼″ (2.04 m). Museo Nazionale, Florence.
b Tony Smith. *Gracehoper.* 1961. Sheet steel, 23 × 22 × 46′ (7.01 × 6.70 × 14.02 m). Detroit Institute of Arts (purchase, donation from W. Hawkins Ferry and Founders Society Funds).
c Piet Mondrian. *Composition London.* 1940–42. Oil on canvas, 32½ × 28″ (83 × 71 cm). Albright-Knox Art Gallery, Buffalo (Room of Contemporary Art Fund).
d Jacob van Ruisdael. *Wheatfields.* c. 1650. Oil on canvas, 3′3⅜″ × 4′3¼″ (1.01 × 1.3 m). Metropolitan Museum of Art, New York (bequest of Benjamin Altman, 1913).

d

Illusion of Space

Size

The easiest way to create an illusion of space or distance is through *size*. Very early in life we all observed the visual phenomenon that as objects get farther away, they appear to become smaller. Thus, when we look at Charpentier's portrait **(a)**, we do not immediately assume that the young woman is a giant Amazon, nor that the other figures are tiny, elfin creatures. Instead, we understand that the small figures are farther from us. In this way a sense of space is established.

In Hobbema's landscape painting **(b)** the repeating forms of the trees gradually diminishing in size effectively lead us back into space, creating a very deep painting with the small-scale town far in the distance.

Notice that the size factor can be effective even with abstract shapes, where there is no literal meaning or representational quality to the forms **(c)**. The smaller squares automatically begin to recede, and we see a spatial pattern. With abstract figures the spatial effect is more pronounced if (as in this case) the same shape is repeated in various sizes. The device works less well with different shapes.

a Constance Marie Charpentier (?). *Mlle. Charlotte du Val-d'Ognes.* c. 1800. Oil on canvas, 5′3½″ × 4′2⅜″ (1.61 × 1.29 m). Metropolitan Museum of Art, New York (bequest of Isaac D. Fletcher, 1917). (Formerly attributed to Jacques Louis David.)

b Meindert Hobbema. *Avenue at Middelharnis.* 1689. Oil on canvas, 3′4¾″ × 4′7½″ (1.04 × 1.41 m). National Gallery, London (reproduced by courtesy of the Trustees).

c If the same shape is repeated in different sizes, a spatial effect can be developed.

a

b

c

Illusion of Space

Hieratic Scaling

Artists in the past often have ignored size as a way to show spatial location. In Egyptian sculpture **(a)** relative size has no connection whatsoever with space. The figure of the Pharaoh is larger not because he is closer to us but because he is more *important* than the other figures. This is called *hieratic scaling*. The size (scale) denotes some conceptual importance, not any visual position in space.

In Hugo van der Goes' painting **(b)** the Madonna is arbitrarily larger than the angels who are spatially closer to us. This shows the importance of the Madonna in the story being told. The shepherds on the right also are large, because the theme of the painting is the *Adoration of the Shepherds*. Size is therefore being used to tell us a story more clearly, not as a spatial device denoting distance.

Meister Francke's painting **(c)** relates the story of *The Pursuit of St. Barbara*. St. Barbara had converted to Christianity, and this enraged her father, who proceeded to lock her up in a

Nonspatial Use of Size

tower. St. Barbara's prayers to the Virgin were answered, and she was flown from the tower and hidden in a forest. Her father pursued her and found her with the help of some shepherds. Angered by the shepherds' treachery, God changed their flocks into grasshoppers. This is a very difficult, complicated story to tell in one image. St. Barbara is shown larger than the trees, but how else would we know she is hiding in the trees? The grasshoppers are greatly enlarged, but if shown in their true scale, they would be tiny dots, and this important part of the story would not be clear to us. Size relationships are spatially confused, but we are much more able to comprehend St. Barbara's plight.

a *King Akhenaten with His Family Sacrificing to Aten.*
New Kingdom, 18th Dynasty, c. 1355 B.C.
From the Aten temple at Tell el Amarna.
Limestone, height 41″ (104 cm). Egyptian Museum, Cairo.
b Hugo van der Goes. *Adoration of the Shepherds,*
detail of *Portinari Altarpiece.* c. 1476. Oil on wood,
entire work 9′2½″ × 21′8½″ (2.81 × 6.62 m). Uffizi, Florence.
c Meister Francke. *The Pursuit of St. Barbara.* c. 1410–15.
Tempera and gesso on plaster, 35½ × 21″ (91 × 54 cm).
National Museum of Finland, Helsinki.

a

b

c

Illusion of Space

Overlapping

Overlapping is a simple device for creating an illusion of depth. When you look at the two rectangles in **a**, you do not assume that the black shape is actually as shown at the right. Instead, you realize that the gray shape is hiding part of the black rectangle because it is on top of or in front of it, thereby automatically creating a sense of depth.

In the detail of Fra Angelico's painting **(b)** the rows of saints are shown with no size difference between the figures in the front row and those in back. But we do understand their respective positions because of the overlapping that hides portions of the figures in the second and third rows. Since overlapping is the only spatial device used, the space created is admittedly very shallow, and we get a "stacked up" feeling. Notice that when overlapping is combined with size differences, as in Perugino's painting **(c)**, the spatial sensation is greatly increased.

The same principle can be illustrated with abstract shapes, as the designs in **d** show. The design at the right, which combines overlapping and size differences, gives a much more effective feeling of spatial recession.

a Overlapping establishes a feeling of depth in a design.
b Fra Angelico. *Christ Glorified in the Court of Heaven*, detail. 1435. Panel, detail 12½ × 25″ (32 × 64 cm). National Gallery, London (reproduced by courtesy of the Trustees).
c Pietro Perugino. *The Delivery of the Keys to St. Peter*. 1482. Fresco. Sistine Chapel, The Vatican, Rome.
d The design at the left does not give so much feeling of spatial depth as the one on the right.

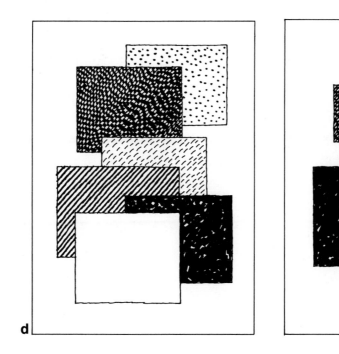

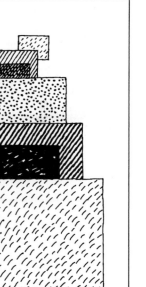

d

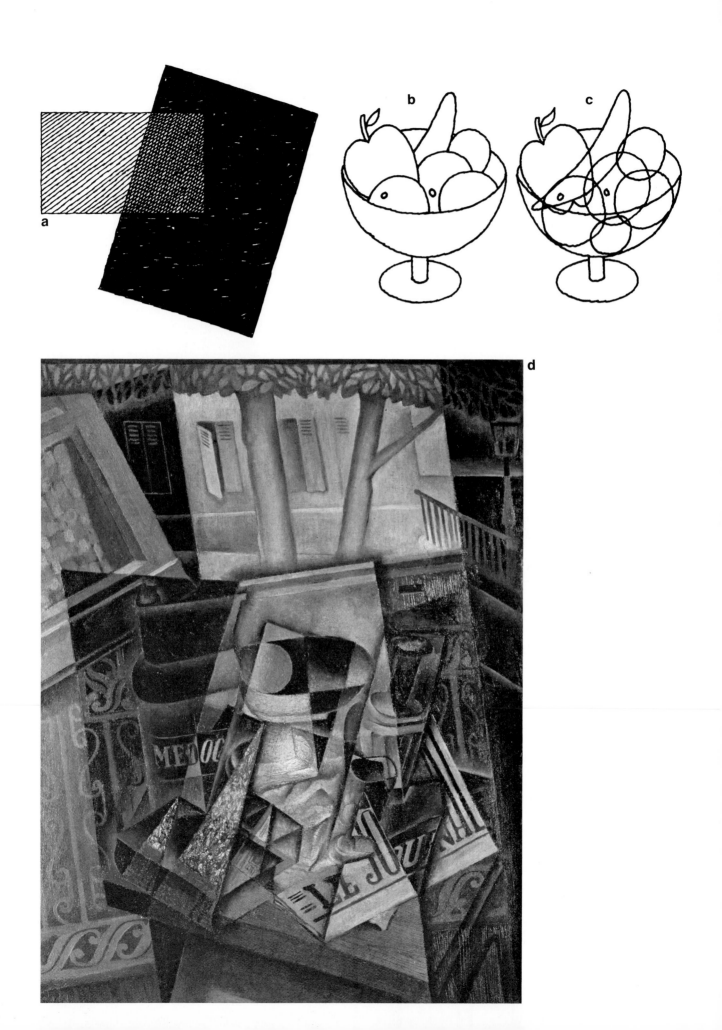

Illusion of Space

Transparency

Many artists in the 20th century have chosen to ignore the device of overlapping. Instead, they have used what is called *transparency.* When two forms overlap and both are seen completely, the figures are assumed to be transparent **(a)**.

Transparency does *not* give us a clear spatial pattern. In **a** we are not sure which form is on top and which behind. The spatial pattern can change as we look at it. This purposeful ambiguity is called *equivocal space,* and many artists find it a more interesting visual pattern than the static spatial clarity that overlapping provides in a design.

There is another rationale for the use of transparency. Just because one item is in front and hides another object does not mean the item in back has ceased to exist. In **b** we see a bowl of fruit depicted with the customary visual device of overlapping. In **c** the same bowl of fruit is shown with transparency, and we discover there are other pieces of fruit in the bot-

tom of the bowl. They were always there but hidden from our view. Which design is more "realistic"? By what standard do you decide?

Cubism was an art style primarily interested in studying form. Therefore, Cubist artists often used transparency **(d)**, because they felt the contrast and relationship of various shapes was more effective if each was seen entirely, instead of being partially hidden by overlapping.

The print by Norman Ives **(e)** is an arrangement of the block shapes of sans-serif letters (letters without decorative tails). However, the use of transparency on all the overlapping letters creates many *new* shapes, and their light and dark changes create an interesting pattern.

a The use of overlapping with transparency confuses our perception of depth.
b Overlapping sometimes can be deceptive.
c The use of transparency reveals what is hidden by overlapping.
d Juan Gris. *Still Life Before an Open Window: Place Ravignan.* 1915. Oil on canvas, 44¾ × 35″ (114 × 89 cm). Philadelphia Museum of Art (Louise and Walter Arensberg Collection).
e Norman Ives. *I: Centaur.* 1973. Serigraph, 7½″ (19 cm) square. Courtesy Ives-Sillman, Inc., Hamden, Conn.

e

Illusion of Space

Vertical Location

Vertical location is a spatial device in which elevation on the page or format indicates a recession into depth. The *higher* an object, the farther back it is assumed to be. In the Persian miniature **(a)** the various figures and objects are depicted with no differences in size but with some overlapping. The artist is relying mainly on vertical location to give us a sense of recession into depth. This spatial device was used widely in Near Eastern art and often in Oriental art **(b)** and was immediately understandable in those cultures.

These examples are charming and decorative, but to our Western eyes they have little spatial depth. To us, the figures appear almost to sit on top of each other all in one plane. How-

ever, if vertical location is combined with a size difference, it provides a very effective feeling of space. In Wyeth's painting **(c)** the distance between the figure and the smaller house is emphatically heightened by the placement of the house at the top of the picture. The isolation of the figure is strongly dramatized by the distance created.

a *Bahram Gur in the Turquoise Palace on Wednesday,*
   Persian miniature. 16th century. Metropolitan Museum of Art,
   New York (gift of Alexander Smith Cochran, 1913).
b Torii Kiyonaga. Scene from the Jōruri play
   An Early Autumn Figure of a Prostitute Flower. c. 1788.
   Color woodcut, 15⅜ × 10⅜″ (39 × 26 cm).
   Nelson-Atkins Gallery, Kansas City (Nelson Fund).
c Andrew Wyeth. *Christina's World.* 1948.
   Tempera on gesso panel, 32¼ × 47¾″ (82 × 121 cm).
   Museum of Modern Art, New York (purchase).

c

Illusion of Space

Vertical Location

Vertical location is based on a visual fact. As we stand and look at a scene before us, the closest place to us is the ground down at our feet. And as we gradually lift our eyes upward, objects gradually move farther away, until we reach what is called the horizon or eye-level (**a**). Thus, a horizon reference is an integral part of vertical location.

Photography has undoubtedly altered our customary view of the world around us. A dramatic photo from a "worm's-eye view" such as **b**, more appropriately termed *amplified perspective*, certainly fits the definition of vertical location. This unusual view makes a dynamic image.

Devices to Show Depth

However, the 20th century also brought us the ability to fly, and we are becoming more and more accustomed to images like **c**. The traditional horizon has disappeared; indeed, now the point farthest from us is near the center of the picture. Therefore, vertical location, while still a useful device in certain circumstances, is not as automatically effective as in the past.

a The location of an object in reference to the eye level helps us establish vertical space.
b World Trade Center, viewed from the base. New York City. © Peter B. Kaplan, 1978.
c Aerial view from Empire State Building, New York City. © Peter B. Kaplan, 1978.

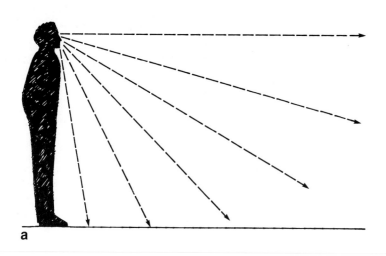

a

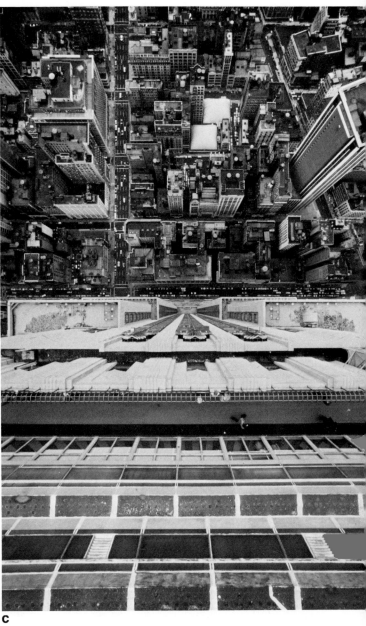

b

c

a

b

c

Illusion of Space

Aerial Perspective

Aerial, or *atmospheric perspective* means the use of color and/or value (dark and light) to show depth. Example **a** illustrates the idea: the value contrast between distant objects gradually lessens, and contours become less distinct. The color would change also, with objects that are far away appearing to be more neutral in color and taking on a bluish character.

In **b** we get a feeling of spatial recession, but it is based entirely on differences in size. Example **c** shows the same design, but the spatial feeling is greatly increased, since the smaller shapes become progressively darker and show less value contrast with the background.

Devices to Show Depth

In the Fausett landscape **(d)** the hills seem to recede far back because of their successively lighter grays—finally almost the same value as the sky. We feel the space and sweep of the valley laid out before us.

A discussion of the spatial effects of various hues appears in "Color and Space" (p. 223).

a Ansel Adams. *Yosemite Valley from Inspiration Point.* Photograph.
b A feeling of spatial recession can be achieved simply by reducing the size of objects as they apparently fade into the distance.
c Spatial recession can be made even more effective if the receding objects blend more and more with the background.
d Dean Fausett. *Derby View.* 1939. Oil tempera on canvas, 24⅛ × 40″ (61 × 102 cm). Museum of Modern Art, New York (purchase from Southern Vermont Artists' Exhibition at Manchester with fund given anonymously).

d

a

b

c

Illusion of Space

Linear Perspective

Linear perspective is a complex spatial system based on a relatively simple visual phenomenon: As parallel lines recede, they appear to converge and to meet on an imaginary line called the *horizon* or *eye level*. We have all noticed this effect with railroad tracks **(a)** or a highway stretching away into the distance. From this obvious visual effect, the whole "science" of linear perspective developed. Artists had long noted this convergence of receding parallel lines, but not until the Renaissance was the idea introduced that parallel lines on parallel planes all converge at the *same* place (a *vanishing point*) on the horizon. Thus, in De Hooch's painting **(b)** all the lines of windows, walls, floor tiles, and ceiling beams, if extended, would meet at a common point **(c)**.

Linear perspective was a dominant device for spatial representation in Western art for several hundred years. It is easy to see why. First, linear perspective does approximate the visual image; it does appear "realistic" for artists

striving to reproduce what the eye sees. Second, by its very nature perspective acts as a unifying factor. With all the lines receding to a common point, it automatically organizes these many trapezoidal shapes into a coherent pattern. Look at Leonardo da Vinci's *The Last Supper* **(d)**. The one-point perspective not only visually unites the two walls, their dark panels, the lines of the coffered ceiling, and so forth, but the vanishing point placed at Christ's head draws our eyes to this focal point. So perfect is this painting in its compositional clarity and absolutely unified spatial organization, that it has become almost a cliché.

a The railroad tracks appear almost to meet far in the distance, near the horizon.
b Pieter de Hooch. *An Interior Scene.* Second half of 17th century. Canvas, 29 × 25⁷⁄₁₆″ (74 × 64 cm). National Gallery, London (reproduced by courtesy of the Trustees).
c The basic structure of the painting in **b** involves all parallel lines converging at the same place.
d Leonardo da Vinci. *The Last Supper.* 1495–98. Fresco, 14′5″ × 28′¼″ (4.39 × 8.54 m). Santa Maria della Grazie, Milan.

d

Illusion of Space

Linear Perspective

The complete study of linear perspective is a complicated task. Whole books are devoted to it alone, and it cannot be fully described here. However, a quick glance at the illustrations will enable you to recognize some different perspective systems.

In the drawing *Urban Blast* **(a)** the tiny figure is about to blow up a vast array of buildings shown in what is referred to as *one-point perspective*. On each of the buildings we can see one side that is parallel to the picture plane, and then the other side diminishes in size as it recedes. All the lines on the different buildings recede to one common vanishing point.

When we look at the corner of a room or building, so that no planes are parallel to the picture plane, *two-point perspective* results. You can see in Canaletto's Venetian scene **(b)** that the lines of the buildings, if extended, would meet at two different, widely spaced vanishing points, one of them outside the picture.

Devices to Show Depth

In Tooker's painting of *The Subway* **(c)** the long, mysterious passageways go back at several different angles. Each recedes to a different point on the horizon line, thereby creating *multipoint perspective*. The painting by Ron Davis **(d)** also uses multipoint perspective—but in an abstract manner.

The rules and "engineering" aspects of linear perspective have led many 20th-century artists away from its use and to reliance on other forms of spatial definition. Linear perspective is merely another tool for artists to employ when appropriate or ignore when they wish.

a Hans-Georg Rauch. *Urban Blast.* Pen and ink drawing. From GRAPHIS, No. 141, 1969, Vol. 25. Courtesy GRAPHIS magazine, Zurich.
b Canaletto. *The Basin of Saint Mark's, Venice.* 1735–41 Oil on canvas, 4 × 6′ (1.21 × 1.83 m). National Gallery, London (reproduced by courtesy of the Trustees).
c George Tooker. *The Subway.* 1950. Tempera on board, 18⅛ × 36⅛″ (46 × 92 cm). Whitney Museum of American Art, New York.
d Ronald Davis. *Frame and Beam.* 1975. Acrylic and dry pigment, 9′4″ × 15′4½″ (2.9 × 4.73 m). Seattle Art Museum (purchased with funds from National Endowment of the Arts, Poncho, and Merrill Foundation).

a

a

b

Illusion of Space

Limitations of Linear Perspective

Linear perspective approximates what our eyes see, but its several limitations have caused it to be less popular in the 20th century than in preceding periods.

Many artists object to the restraints perspective implies. The artist's compositional freedom consists of the placement of the horizon, vanishing points, and the first line. From that point the composition becomes a mechanical drawing exercise in following rules.

The main objection is the "frozen" quality that linear perspective imparts. With the necessarily unchanging horizon line and vanishing points, a perspective drawing suggests a stoppage of time; we are staring at a scene without movement. This is not what we experience in life, for our visual knowledge is gained by looking at objects or scenes from many changing viewpoints. Example **a** is a photo of a room from

Devices to Show Depth

a fixed viewpoint—a "true" view if we came in, stopped completely, and stared at the room without even moving our eyes. This, however, is a limited perspective and not true-to-life. In **b**, a composite photo, the camera was focused on several parts of the room individually and the results combined into one composition. This image much more approximates our visual experience as our eyes move from one item to another, looking at each in turn.

This changing aspect of perception is obviously what Renato Guttuso was attempting in **c**. Rather than taking one fixed view, the artist shows different figures from different angles to suggest the effect of moving along a beach.

a Linear perspective can show only one viewpoint at one moment.
b In reality, our eyes move from one object to another, combining many images to make a composite whole.
c Renato Guttuso. *The Beach*. 1955. Oil on canvas, 9'9⅜" × 14'8¼" (3.01 × 4.52 m). Galleria Nazionale, Parma.

c

Illusion of Space

To introduce a dramatic, dynamic quality into their pictures, many artists have used what is called *amplified perspective*. This device reproduces the visual image, but in a very special view that occurs when an item is pointed directly at the viewer.

A familiar example is James Montgomery Flagg's recruiting poster of Uncle Sam **(a)**, in which the pointing finger is thrust right at the viewer and the arm recedes sharply. This effect is called *foreshortening*. Because the arm points right at us, it looks "shorter" than we know it to be. In profile, of course, the arm would look much longer.

In Dali's crucifixion **(b)** the body of Christ is also foreshortened. We look from above the cross, so that the body very quickly recedes down and away from us, rapidly getting smaller. It is an unusual view, and the size contrast of large to small is pictorially exciting.

Another advantage to amplified perspective is that the viewer's eye is pulled into the picture. In Caravaggio's painting **(c)**, St. Paul's fallen body thrust diagonally at us exerts a dynamic pull inward, avoiding the rather static, frozen quality of so many works. With amplified perspective, the spatial quality itself becomes the image's most eye-catching element. It is an effective tool in making the viewer forget the picture is a flat, two dimensional plane.

a James Montgomery Flagg. *I Want YOU*. World War I recruiting poster. Library of Congress, Washington, D.C.
b Salvador Dali. *Christ of St. John of the Cross*. 1951. Oil on canvas, 6'8⅝" × 3'9⅝" (2.05 × 1.16 m). Glasgow Art Gallery (purchased 1952).
c Caravaggio. *The Conversion of St. Paul*. 1601. Oil on canvas, 7'6" × 5'8¼" (2.3 × 1.75 m). Santa Maria del Popolo, Rome.

a

I WANT YOU
FOR U.S. ARMY
NEAREST RECRUITING STATION

b

c

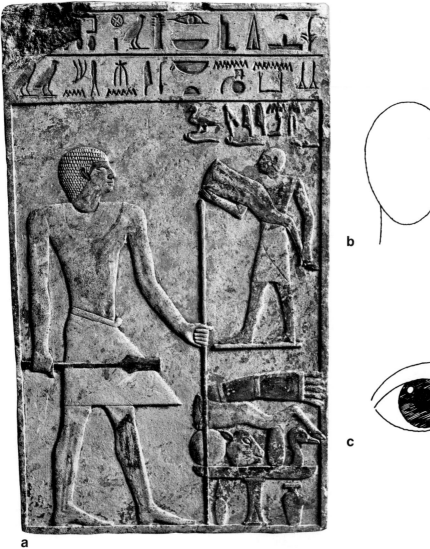

a

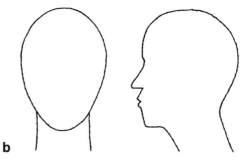

b

c

d

Illusion of Space

Multiple Perspective

Looking at a figure or object from more than one vantage point simultaneously is called *multiple perspective*. Several different views are combined in one image. This device has been used widely in 20th-century art, although the idea is centuries old.

Multiple perspective was a basic pictorial device in Egyptian art, as illustrated in a typical Egyptian relief figure **(a)**. The artist's aim was not necessarily to reproduce the visual image, but rather to give a composite image combining the most descriptive or characteristic view of each part of the body. In **b**, which view of the head is most descriptive, which most certainly a head? The profile obviously says "head" more clearly. But what about the eye **(c)**? The eye in profile is a confusing shape, whereas the front view is what we know as an eye. The Egyptians solved this problem by combining a side view of the head with a front view of the eye. Each body part is thus presented in its most characteristic aspect: a front view of the torso, a side view of the legs, and so forth.

The Egyptian painting of a garden pool **(d)** shows the same approach. A pool is most clearly a rectangular shape from a top view, but do trees look like trees from the top? The typical tree structure is best seen from the side. Also, fish and birds from above would hardly be recognizable. The solution is not a unified view from one vantage point, but a composite—a clearly readable (and charming) image.

Multiple perspective was widely used also in Near Eastern and Indian art. Notice the pool and fountain in the Indian picture **(e)**.

a *Priest of Osiris.* Egyptian, Middle Kingdom, 12th dynasty. Relief. Museo Barracco, Rome.
b To the Egyptians, the head shown in profile seemed to be the most characteristic view.
c The *front* view of the eye gives the clearest, most descriptive view.
d *A Pool in a Garden.* Fragment of a wall painting from the tomb of Nebamun, Thebes. c. 1400 B.C. Distemper. British Museum, London (reproduced by courtesy of the Trustees).
e *Ladies in a Pleasure Garden,* detail. Manuscript illumination from Bundi, India. c. 1675–1700. 12 × 8¾″ (30 × 22 cm). Prince of Wales Museum, Bombay.

e

Illusion of Space

While not attempting to emulate the Egyptians, many artists in the 20th century have made use of multiple perspective. With the camera now able to give us effortlessly the fixed visual ("realistic") view, artists have been freed to explore other avenues of perception.

The Cubist artist Braque clearly employed multiple perspective in his still-life **(a)**. We look down on the top of the table to see more clearly the items collected there. But the table itself is as important as the objects (the picture is entitled *The Round Table*), and it would be a pity not to see the delightful old-fashioned base and curved legs. So we see them from the side. The still-life items themselves, while *abstracted* or simplified into basic shapes, are shown from differing angles to give us the most descriptive view, or views, of each individual item.

In Picasso's painting *The Dream* **(b)** we see the subject's head both in profile and in front-face. Again the form has been highly simplified. The objective here is not an individual portrait of a specific person, but rather a conceptual image of a head. Heads *are* seen in life in various positions from different angles.

As you have noticed, multiple perspective does not give us a clear spatial pattern of the position occupied by each element. This aspect has been sacrificed to give a more subjective, conceptual view of forms.

a Georges Braque. *The Round Table.* 1929. Oil on canvas, 4'10" × 3'9" (1.47 × 1.14 m). Phillips Collection, Washington, D.C.
b Pablo Picasso. *The Dream.* 1932. Oil on canvas, 4'4" × 3'3" (1.32 × .99 m). Collection Mr. and Mrs. Victor W. Ganz, New York.

a

b

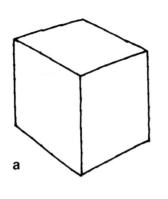

a

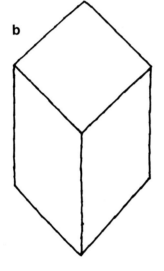

b

c

d

Illusion of Space

Isometric Projection

For centuries, Oriental artists did not make wide use of linear perspective. They had another spatial convention satisfactory for their pictorial purposes. In Oriental art planes recede on the diagonal, but the lines, instead of drawing closer together, remain parallel. Example **a** shows a box drawn in linear perspective, **b** the box drawn in the Oriental method. In the West, we refer to an image like **b** as an isometric projection.

A typical Japanese print **(c)** illustrates this device. The effect is different, but certainly not disturbing. For one thing, the space is already very shallow; the corner of the room is not far from the picture plane. The rather flat decorative effect seems perfectly in keeping with the treatment of the figures, with their strong linear patterns and flat color areas. The artist does not stress three-dimensional solidity or roundness in the figures, so we do not miss it in the background.

In fact, when linear perspective *is* used by an Oriental artist, as in **d**, the effect can be quite unsatisfactory. The same flat figures now look strange in a deep space—rather like the pop-up figures in children's books.

Oriental art rarely stressed the strictly visual impression of the world. The art was more subjective, more evocative than descriptive of the natural world. Linear perspective was undoubtedly not needed for the expressive aims of these artists.

Today isometric projection is used extensively in engineering and mechanical drawings, but not so often in art. Artists occasionally do work in isometric projection, as in the self-portrait by David Hockney **(e)**. This change from the more common linear perspective is unexpected and intriguing.

a In linear perspective, parallel lines gradually draw closer together as they recede in the distance.
b In isometric projection, parallel lines remain parallel.
c Suzuki Harunobu. *Justice, Righteousness,* from the series *The Five Cardinal Virtues.* Second half of 18th century. Woodcut, 11¼ × 8½″ (20 × 22 cm). Private collection.
d Furuyama Moromasa. *Game of Hand Sūmo.* c. 1740. Woodcut, 13 × 18½″ (33 × 47 cm). Metropolitan Museum of Art, New York (purchase, Frederick Charles Hewitt Bequest Income, 1912).
e David Hockney *Self-Portrait with Blue Guitar.* 1977. Oil on canvas, 5 × 6′ (1.52 × 1.83 m). Collection Dr. Peter Ludwig, Aachen, West Germany.

Illusion of Space

Open Form/Closed Form

One other aspect of pictorial space is of concern to the artist or designer. This is the concept of *enclosure*—the use of what is referred to as *open form* or *closed form*. The artist has the choice of giving us a complete scene or merely a partial glimpse in which we see only a portion of a scene that continues beyond the format. In **a** Fragonard has enclosed the focal point, and our eyes are not led out of the painting. The inward-facing statue and the mass of trees at left frame the lovers in the center and effectively keep our attention focused on them. This is called *closed form*.

By contrast, Degas' racetrack scene **(b)** is clearly *open form*. A horse gallops onto the canvas from the left, and a carriage disappears off the right edge with one gentleman barely making it into the picture.

Clayton Pond's humorous serigraph **(c)**, called *Self-Portrait in the Bathtub*, is the essence of open form. In fact, it almost forces us to think more of the parts we *cannot* see than of those shown in the picture.

The ultimate extension of the open form concept is illustrated in **d**. This large, nonobjective painting by Jasper Johns has a shape that in reality *does* protrude outside the rectangle of the painting. The shape both surprises us and effectively destroys any "framed" or contained feeling in the format.

As you can see, closed form generally gives a rather formal, structured appearance, whereas open form creates a casual, momentary feeling with elements moving on and off the format in an informal manner.

a Jean-Honoré Fragonard. *The Love Letters*. 1771-73. Oil on canvas, 10′4⅛″ × 7′1⅜″ (3.17 × 2.17 m). Frick Collection, New York.
b Edgar Degas. *At the Races*. 1877–80. Oil on canvas, 26 × 32½″ (66 × 83 cm). Louvre, Paris.
c Clayton Pond. *Self-Portrait in the Bathtub*, from the series *Things in My Studio*. 1973. Serigraph, 23 × 29″ (58 × 74 cm). Courtesy Associated American Artists, New York.
d Jasper Johns. *Studio*. 1964. Oil on canvas, 6′1½″ × 12′1½″ (1.87 × 3.70 m). Whitney Museum of American Art, New York (gift of the Friends of the Whitney Museum and purchase).

a

b

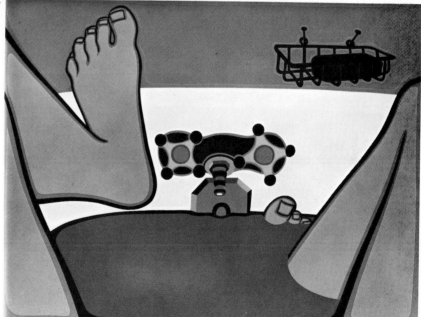

c

d

a

b

c

Illusion of Space

Artists all learn the various devices to give an illusion of depth or space. At times, however, certain artists purposely have ignored these conventions to provide an unexpected image. A confusion of spatial relationships is intriguing, because the viewer is confronted with a visual puzzle rather than a statement.

Piranesi in one of his many etchings of prisons **(a)** does not merely ignore the "rules" but actually distorts them to create a wierd, spatially intricate scene. The confused, mazelike complexity of the enormous chamber serves as an ominous symbol of government bureaucracy and repression.

The English artist William Hogarth called his etching *A Perspective Joke* **(b)**. This humorous image contains all sorts of elements that destroy our initial impression of the scene. Absolutely impossible spatial things happen, and the more we look, the more nonsensical spatial incongruities we can find. The contemporary artist David Hockney has taken elements from this Hogarth etching for a work **(c)** that retains much of the spatial ambiguity.

Spatial Puzzles

Example **d** is a Surrealist painting. The whole thrust of Surrealism was to illustrate the impossible world of dreams and the subconscious mind. In **d**, René Magritte gives us a truly strange painting. We are outside a building looking in a window, and the scene *inside* is another exterior. There is no way to explain it logically; we experience it for this strangeness.

The brilliance of M. C. Escher's draughtsmanship is shown in his lithograph *Waterfall* **(e)**. We cannot detect any mistakes in the perspective. And yet, what appears to be a perfectly straightforward scene suddenly becomes an impossible spatial situation.

a Giovanni Battista Piranesi. *The Prisons.* c. 1750. Etching, 21⅜ × 16¼″ (54 × 41 cm). Metropolitan Museum of Art, New York (Harris Brisbane Dick Fund, 1937).
b William Hogarth. *A Perspective Joke.* 1754. Etching, 8¼ × 6¾″ (21× 17 cm).
c David Hockney. *Kirby (after Hogarth) Useful Knowledge.* 1975. Oil on canvas, 6′ × 5⅛″ (1.83 × 1.53 m). Museum of Modern Art, New York (purchase and gift of the artist and J. Kasmin).
d René Magritte. *In Praise of Dialectics.* 1937. Oil on canvas, 25⅛ × 21″ (65 × 54 cm). National Gallery of Victoria, Melbourne, Australia (Felton Bequest, 1972).
e M. C. Escher. *Waterfall.* 1961. Lithograph, 14⅞ × 11¾″ (38 × 30 cm). Escher Foundation, Gemeentemuseum, The Hague.

d

e

Illusion of Motion

a

b

Illusion of Motion

Introduction

Examples **a** and **b** are completely different forms of visual art: they were produced by very different artists in very different societies in different centuries for very different purposes. Yet they share one common basic aim. Both are attempting to portray a feeling of *movement* by showing a series of images that imply motion and a passage of time between episodes.

In a comic strip such as **a**, we follow a character through a series of situations that relate a story. But **b** has the same idea, though the format is not broken into separate panels. In Sassetta's painting, we see the main character, St. Anthony, in three situations. At upper left he embarks on his travels; at upper right he encounters a centaur, which he blesses; in the closest area at lower right he ultimately arrives at his meeting with St. Paul, whom he embraces. Very dissimilar images have the same goal—an illusion of motion.

Some art forms involve *actual* motion. In life, when we look at a mobile by Calder **(c)**, we see real movement. The form presents a constantly changing visual pattern of shapes. The relationship of forms is always shifting and making new designs—unlike the situation in this photograph, which shows only one aspect with the movement stopped. In observing any of the three-dimensional arts, such as sculpture and architecture, much of the visual interest has always come from our moving about and looking at the object from different angles. But when the piece of art itself moves, we apply to it the term *kinetic*. Kinetic sculpture moves although we ourselves may stand still.

a Pogo cartoon from TEN EVER-LOVIN' BLUE-EYED YEARS WITH POGO by Walt Kelly (New York: Simon & Schuster). Copyright © 1959 by Walt Kelly.

b Sassetta. *Meeting of St. Anthony and St. Paul the Hermit.* 1430–32. Panel, 18¾ × 13⅝″ (48 × 35 cm). National Gallery of Art, Washington, D.C. (Samuel H. Kress Collection).

c Alexander Calder. *Sumac.* 1961. Hanging mobile, sheet metal and steel wire; 4′1¾″ × 7′10″ (1.26 × 2.39 m). Courtesy Perls Gallery, New York.

c

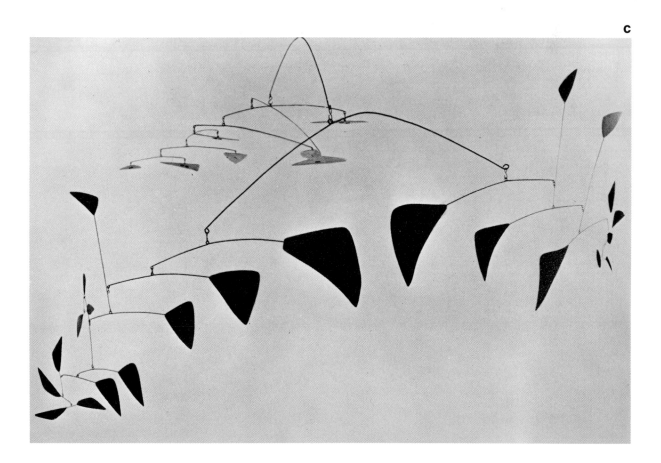

Illusion of Motion

Introduction

There have been many attempts to inject some feeling of motion into the essentially static images of two-dimensional drawing and painting. In this case, the movement is merely an illusion, a suggestion where no actual motion is possible. Why do artists attempt this illusion of motion, a quality that patently cannot be present? The reason is that change and movement are essential characteristics of our world. We humans cannot sit or stand motionless for more than a moment or so; even in sleep we turn and change position. But if we could stop our body movements, the world about us would still continue to change.

Ever since prehistoric times this dynamic quality of our world has been noticed. When the Paleolithic cave dwellers first drew pictures on their cave walls, their images of animals were often portrayed with the front and rear legs extended in positions of movement **(a)**. These primitive artists recognized an essential characteristic of animals: they run and move. Many subsequent artists also have attempted to reflect this idea **(b)**.

Presenting an illusion of motion is, like most aspects of art, an option for the artist. Some artists strive for it; others purposely ignore it. In periods of art that are commonly styled *classical*, the whole concept of motion is consciously rejected. Here, art strives for unemo-

tional, reserved images that have an ageless, permanent quality. A suggestion of anything momentary or temporary is rejected. The idealized forms exude an air of unchanging stability, devoid of motion. The Raphael painting in **c** is an example of this approach. Raphael's exquisitely graceful, relaxed figures are posed in an idyllic landscape. No hint of change disturbs their serenity.

The painting by Rubens in **d** is clearly very different. Here everything about the subject suggests a momentary quality. One moment before and one moment later the positions, and hence the whole visual pattern, would have been entirely different. The theme of Prometheus, the action poses, the amplified perspective, even the stormy background all combine to capture a single moment in the struggle.

a *Hall of Bulls,* left wall, Lascaux. c. 15,000–10,000 B.C. Dordogne, France.
b Giacomo Balla. *Dog on a Leash.* 1912. Oil on canvas, 35⅜ × 43¼″ (90 × 110 cm). Albright-Knox Art Gallery, Buffalo (Courtesy George F. Goodyear and the Buffalo Fine Arts Academy).
c Raphael. *The Alba Madonna.* c. 1511. Oil on panel transferred to canvas, diameter 37¼″ (95 cm). National Gallery of Art, Washington, D.C. (Andrew Mellon Collection).
d Peter Paul Rubens. *Prometheus Bound.* 1611–12. Oil on canvas, 7′11⅛″ × 6′10½″ (2.44 × 2.1 m). Philadelphia Museum of Art (purchase, W. P. Wilstach Collection).

a

b

c

d

Illusion of Motion

Memory Images

Much of the implication of movement present in art is caused by our memory images. We recognize temporary, unstable body positions and realize that change is imminent. We immediately "see" the action portrayed in a section from the Bayeux Tapestry **(a)**. From the positions of the bodies and the horses, we know that quite violent movement is taking place.

A feeling of movement can be heightened by contrast. Again, by memory we realize that some things move and some do not. Thus, in an image like **b**, the figures seem to have more activity, more potential of movement in their active positions, because of the contrast with the large, stolid building that appears so immobile. Our experience tells us that people move, buildings rarely do.

Even nonobjective patterns can display movement in this way. Also because of memory association, we see horizontal lines as quiet and inactive, just as our bodies are resting and still

when we are lying horizontally. For a similar reason we identify diagonal lines as suggestions of movement, as our bodies lean and bend in action-filled activities like sports. The horizontal emphasis of the building in **b** lends it a static feeling. But pure lines without subject reference give the same result. Thus, Mondrian's paintings, with their constant repetition of stabilizing horizontal and vertical lines, seem static and unmoving. In contrast, a painting such as **c** is a dynamic, motion-filled image solely because of the emphasis on diagonal movement and vigorous brushstrokes.

a *Climax of the Battle of Hastings*, detail of *Bayeux Tapestry*. c. 1073–88. Wool embroidery on linen; height 20″ (51 cm), overall length 231′ (70.41 m). Town Hall, Bayeux.

b Nicolas Poussin. *Rape of the Sabine Woman*. c. 1636–37. Oil on canvas, 5′1″ × 6′10½″ (1.55 × 2.1 m). Metropolitan Museum of Art, New York (Harris Brisbane Dick Fund).

c Michael Larionov. *Rayonist Composition: Domination of Red*. 1912–13. Oil on canvas, 20¾ × 28½″ (53 × 72 cm). Museum of Modern Art, New York (gift of the artist).

a

a

b

Illusion of Motion

Figure Repeated

Over the centuries, artists have devised various conventions for presenting an illusion of motion in art. One of the oldest devices is that of repeating a figure. As the Indian miniature in **a** illustrates, the figure of Krishna appears over and over in different positions and situations. This device was used widely in western Medieval art **(b)**, as well as in most Oriental cultures. It is interesting to note that this very old technique is still popular. Any time a figure is repeated, as in the double-image portrait in **c**, a feeling of movement results.

Often, the repeated figure, rather than being shown in a sequence of small pictures, merely reappears in one unified composition. This device also occurred in Oriental art, was adopted in Western art, and remained popular as late as the Renaissance. Usually, a distinctive costume

or color identified the repeated character, so the repetition would be visually obvious. The effect can be quite subtle, as in *The Tribute Money* by Masaccio **(d)**, painted about 1427. The tax collector demands the tribute money of Christ in the center, as Christ tells Peter to get the money from the fish's mouth. On the left Peter kneels to get the money, and on the right he pays it to the tax collector. Without more than casual observation, however, we might miss the important sequential aspect.

a *Krishna Revealing His Nature as Vishnu.* Miniature from Malwa, India. c. 1730. Victoria & Albert Museum, London (Crown Copyright).
b Scenes from the life of St. Paul, from the *Bible of Charles the Bald.* c. 875–77. Illumination. St. Paul Outside the Walls, Rome.
c Alex Katz. *Face of a Poet.* 1972. Oil on canvas, 9′6″ × 17′6″ (2.9 × 5.33 m). Collection Paul Jacques Schupf, New York.
d Masaccio. *The Tribute Money.* c. 1427. Fresco, 8′4″ × 19′8″ (2.54 × 5.99 m). Santa Maria del Carmine, Florence.

a

b

c

Illusion of Motion

We readily interpret a photograph like the one in **a** as a symbol of movement. With a fast shutter speed, moving images are frozen into "stop-action" photographs. Here the shutter speed is relatively slow, so that the sprinting commuter becomes a blurred, indistinct image that we read as an indication of the subject's movement. This is an everyday visual experience. When objects move through our field of vision quickly, we do not get a clear mental picture of them. A car will pass us on the highway so fast that we perceive only a colored blur. Details and edges of the form are lost in the rapidity of movement.

The two figures in the drawing by the artist Daumier **(b)** suggest movement in this same way. They are drawn with sketchy, incomplete, and overlapping lines to define the forms. The figure behind the rail literally wags his finger at the startled lawyer. The hand appears in rapid movement, for we get no one clear view in the blur of motion.

The painting by Renoir in **c** offers an excellent suggestion of motion in the dancing figures and the flicker of gas lamps in a 19th-century dance hall. This movement results mainly from the lack of clear contour lines around the forms. The figures are slightly fuzzy, and many of the forms begin to merge without clear dividing edges.

Even in purely nonobjective paintings, the blurred edge serves as an effective device. The vertical, sweeping shapes in **d** clearly suggest rapid movement.

a Elliott Erwitt. *Commuter*. 1964. Photograph.
b Honoré Daumier. *A Criminal Case*. Pen and ink and black chalk, 7⅛ × 11¼" (18 × 29 cm). Victoria & Albert Museum, London (Crown Copyright).
c Auguste Renoir. *Le Moulin de la Galette*. 1876. Oil on canvas, 4'3½" × 5'9" (1.31 × 1.75 m). Louvre, Paris.
d Morris Louis. *Saraband*. 1959. Acrylic on canvas, 8'6" × 12'5" (2.57 × 3.78 m). Solomon R. Guggenheim Museum, New York.

d

Illusion of Motion

Multiple Image

Another device for suggesting movement is called *multiple image,* as illustrated in **a**. When we see one figure in an overlapping sequence of poses, the slight change in each successive position suggests movement taking place. Example **a** is an old photograph dating from the 1880s. The photographer, Thomas Eakins, was intrigued with the camera's capabilities for answering the visual problem of showing movement and analyzing it.

Example **b** shows this idea in a drawing by Ingres. While Ingres' motive was probably just to try two different positions for the figure, the effect we get is a clear suggestion of the figure moving in dancelike gestures.

The Futurist painters of the early part of the 20th century were primarily concerned with finding a visual language to express the movement and dynamic quality of the world around us. Futurism adopted this multiple-image device for painting, although with freer, less exact images than those captured by the camera. Example **c** is a painting by Balla called *Girl Running Along a Balcony.* We recognize several

images of the girl; in particular, the repetition of the feet in various positions clearly suggests the movement of the figure across the canvas. Dark vertical lines show the balcony railing that disappears and reappears as the figure crosses our field of vision. This painting combines the multiple-image idea with the technique of omitting clear contour lines around each image.

The familiar Venus figure from Botticelli's painting **(d)** has been presented in a new way by Jiří Kolář **(e)**. Using the multiple image in a unique manner, he repeats parts of the figure over and over in a vertical sequence. The visual effect is a feeling of movement.

a Thomas Eakins. *Pole-Vaulter: Multiple Exposure Photograph of George Reynolds.* c. 1884. Metropolitan Museum of Art, New York (gift of Charles Bregler, 1941).
b Jean Auguste Dominique Ingres. *Female Nude.* Pencil on white paper. Musée Bonnat, Bayonne.
c Giacomo Balla. *Girl Running Along a Balcony.* Oil on canvas, 4'¾" (1.25 m) square. Civica Galleria d'Arte Moderna, Milan.
d Sandro Botticelli. *The Birth of Venus,* detail. c. 1480. Oil on canvas, 5'8⅞" × 9'1⅞" (1.75 × 2.79 m). Uffizi, Florence.
e Jiří Kolář. *Venus.* 1968. Rollage. Courtesy the artist.

a

b

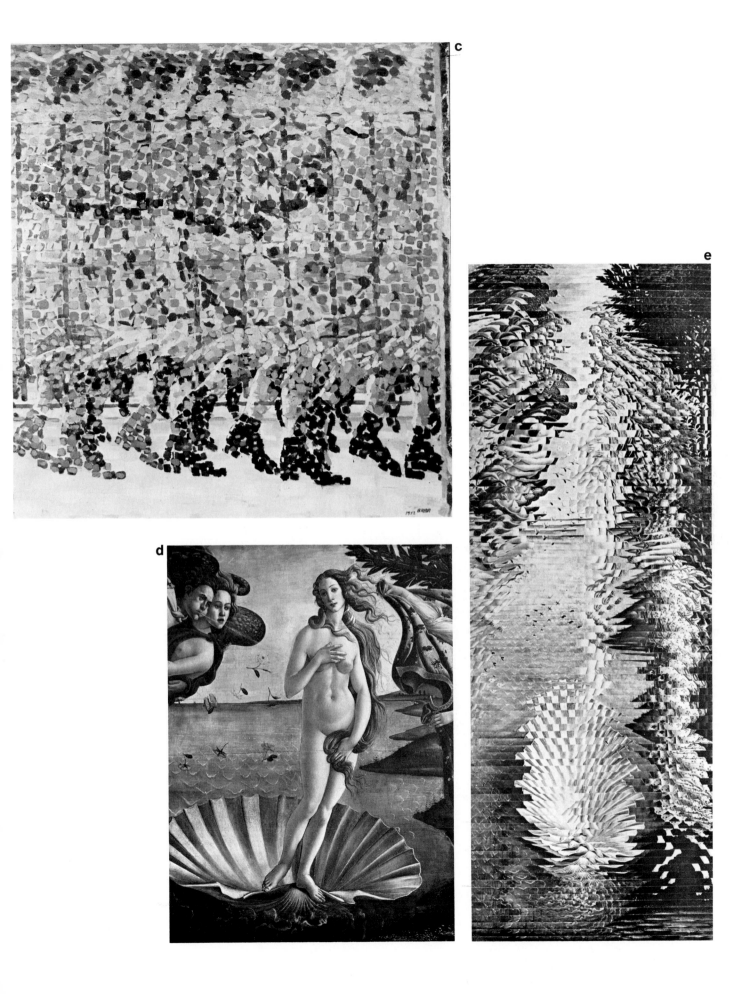

c

e

d

Illusion of Motion

Optical Movement

The paintings illustrated on these pages could scarcely be more different in almost every aspect of art. But again, they have one element in common. All attempt to give an illusion of motion by *optical movement*. The visual pattern presented literally forces our eyes to keep moving about the painting. This constant eye movement encourages us to feel the dynamic quality inherent in each image.

Rubens in his painting **(a)** gives us a very complicated, twisting and curving linear structure. Contour lines are fairly clear, but they make an extremely busy pattern. Figures bend and gesture wildly, the horse rears up and paws the air, Cupid flies in, a bright red cape flutters out, clouds gather; nowhere is the eye really allowed to pause.

In the Rubens painting the momentary positions of all the figures reinforce the feeling of motion. In **b** there are no recognizable objects, no forms that we can identify as being in

fleeting positions. Yet the same optical movement factor is present and perhaps more obvious because of this painting's nonobjective nature. Example **b**, a work by de Kooning, is an example of Abstract Expressionism (so aptly subtitled Action Painting), which took movement and dynamic excitement as a primary goal. The eye is moved rapidly around the canvas. Moreover, we instantly sense the physical activity of the artist in creating the painting. In **c,** the twisting and writhing forms force the eye to wander around the contours, observing the continuous movement of intertwining human and mythological figures.

a Peter Paul Rubens. *Rape of the Daughters of Leucippus.*
c. 1618. Oil on canvas, 7′3″ × 6′10″ (2.22 × 2.09 m).
Alte Pinakothek, Munich.
b Willem de Kooning. *Composition.* 1955.
Oil on canvas, 6′7⅛″ × 5′9⅛″ (2.01 × 1.76 m).
Solomon R. Guggenheim Museum, New York.
c Initial *A* from Manuscript of Josephus.
Canterbury, early 12th century. University Library, Cambridge.

c

Illusion of Motion

Op Art

One recent style in art again concentrated on the idea of movement but in totally nonobjective terms. This style was popularly called *Op Art,* since the images appealed mainly to the eye and involved the retina, not the brain or memory. The patterns were often what we commonly term optical *illusions*—in this case illusions of movement in static images. Op Art paintings are simple, repetitive patterns of definite, hard-edge, often geometric shapes. In theory such elements should not suggest movement. But the hard edges begin to blur, soften, and "swim" before our eyes. Colors vibrate and glow like neon. The flat canvas even appears to undulate and become a billowing, rippling surface. Staring for just a few moments at Bridget Riley's *Current* **(a)** reveals the way the design seems to move and change.

Op Art works involve no recognizable subject matter, often no color, no blurred painted

forms, no dynamic brushstrokes—and yet the image actually *does* change. This is an illusion, of course, but certainly an effective one. Many Op Art images can rather quickly cause actual optical strain. The energy-filled illusion is fascinating, but we need to look away to escape optical discomfort.

Stare at the center of the concentric circles in Tadasky's painting in **b**. Suddenly a black line begins to whirl back and forth like a propeller turning on the pattern. A dynamic element not present in the painting appears before our eyes.

a Bridget Riley. *Current.* 1964. Synthetic polymer paint on board, 4'10⅜" × 4'10⅞" (1.48 × 1.5 m). Museum of Modern Art, New York (Philip C. Johnson Fund).
b Tadasky (Tadasuke Kuwayama). *A-101.* 1964. Synthetic polymer paint on canvas, 4'4" (1.32 m) square. Museum of Modern Art, New York (Larry Aldrich Foundation Fund).

a

b

Rhythm

a

b

Rhythm

Introduction

Rhythm is a principle we associate with the sense of hearing. Music, without words, can intrigue us by its pulsating beat, inducing us to tap a foot or perhaps dance. Poetry often has *meter,* which is another term for rhythm. The pace of words can establish a cadence, a repetitive flow of syllables that makes reading poems aloud a pleasure. We also speak of the rhythm in movement displayed by athletes, dancers, and some workers performing manual tasks. And, of course, rhythm is a basic characteristic of nature. The successive pattern of the seasons, of day and night, and of the tides, even the movement of the planets in the universe—all exhibit a regular rhythm.

This same quality of rhythm can be applied to the visual arts, where the idea of rhythm is basically related to movement. Here the concept refers to the movement of the viewer's eye, a movement across recurrent motifs providing the regularity inherent in the idea of rhythm. Often in conversation we loosely apply the term "rhythmic" to any visual pattern that causes the eye to move quickly and easily from one element to another. But rhythm as a design principle is based on repetition. Repetition, as an element of visual unity, is exhibited in some manner by almost every work of art. However, rhythm involves a clear repetition of elements that are the same or only slightly modified. Just as in music, some visual rhythms can be *legato,* or connecting and flowing; others are *staccato,* or abrupt and dynamic. The watercolor in **a** would be called rhythmic. Repeated jagged, triangular shapes are the dominant elements of the composition and establish a visual rhythm of repetition.

Example **b** is a cast photograph of the musical, *A Chorus Line.* The lined-up figures create a horizontal band of repeating elements across the format. Against the dark background the occasional light spots on some figures develop a rhythm, like the accented beat in music.

a John Marin. *Lower Manhattan.* 1920. Watercolor, 21⅞ × 26¾″ (56 × 68 cm). Museum of Modern Art, New York (Philip L. Goodwin Collection).
b Herbert Migdoll, designer, art director, and photographer. *A Chorus Line* souvenir program, four-page center foldout showing cast. Published by New York Shakespeare Festival.

Rhythm

We can speak of the rhythmic repetition of colors or textures, but most often we think of rhythm in the context of shapes. The painting in **a** has small, dark squares that move in a staccato pattern horizontally and vertically around the canvas. It is the recurrence of this motif that establishes a visual rhythm. The irregular spacing of these small squares causes the pattern (and rhythm) to be lively, rather than monotonous. The artist, Piet Mondrian, titled this painting *Broadway Boogie-Woogie.* He has expressed in the most abstract of visual terms not only the on/off patterns of Broadway's neon landscape, but also the rhythmic sounds of 1940s instrumental blues music.

The title *Nude Descending a Staircase* would identify the painting in **b** as one concerned

with movement. But even without the title, the rhythm of the repetitive shapes would be immediately noticed. The planes of the abstracted body forms are repeated diagonally down the canvas. Countless triangular forms of the legs create a sequence of recurrent shapes. These triangles of the moving legs vary considerably in shape, but the repetition provides a definite rhythmic pattern.

a Piet Mondrian. *Broadway Boogie-Woogie.* 1942–43. Oil on canvas, 4′2″ (1.27 m) square. Museum of Modern Art, New York.
b Marcel Duchamp. *Nude Descending a Staircase, No. 2.* 1912. Oil on canvas, 4′10″ × 2′11″ (1.47 × .89 m). Philadelphia Museum of Art (Louise and Walter Arensberg Collection).

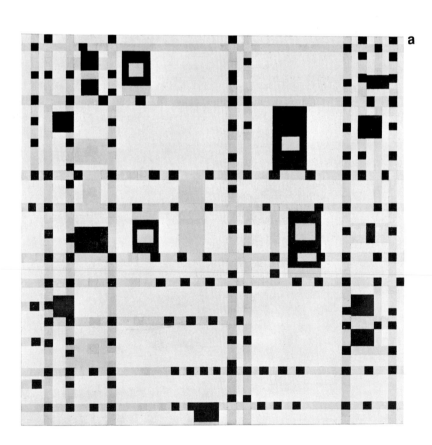

a

NU DESCENDANT UN ESCALIER

b

a

b

Rhythm

There is a special type of rhythm that involves repetition in a slightly different way. When we look at a colonnaded Grecian temple **(a)**, with its repeating pattern of light columns and darker negative spaces, we say that the visual pattern is rhythmic. Here the design is an *alternating* rhythm—a rhythm of two motifs that alternate with one another to produce a regular (and soon anticipated) sequence. This expected quality of the pattern is not a fault, for unless the repetition is fairly obvious, the whole idea of visual rhythm becomes obscure.

The repetitive effect of the knobby vertical linear elements in Jackson Pollock's *Blue Poles* **(b)** gives a similar rhythmic pattern, albeit a freer, less rigidly regular one. The main difference here is that the intervening alternate areas are not simple negative spaces. Instead, these areas are filled with incredibly busy, complicated pat-

terns of dribbled, spattered paint so typical of Pollock's work. If the vertical "poles" continued from top to bottom of the format, they probably would function as negative, rather than positive, elements.

The same quality can be seen in **c**, a painting by Jacob Lawrence. In this work tall, vertical, triangular shapes of the train seats move rhythmically across the painting, alternating with the abstracted, generally drooping, tired figures of the train's passengers.

a Theseum (Hephaestum), Athens. Begun 449 B.C.
b Jackson Pollock. *Blue Poles.* 1952. Mixed media, 6'11½" × 16'½" (2.12 × 4.89 m). Australian National Gallery, Canberra.
c Jacob Lawrence. *Going Home.* 1946. Gouache, 21½ × 29½" (55 × 75 cm). Collection IBM Corporation.

c

146

Rhythm

Another type of rhythm is called *progression,* or *progressive rhythm.* Again the rhythm involves repetition, but in this case repetition of a shape that *changes* in a regular manner. There is a feeling of a sequential pattern. This type of rhythm is most often achieved with a progressive variation of the size of a shape, though its color, value, or texture could be the varying element. Progressive rhythm is extremely familiar to us; we experience it daily. Every time we look at buildings from an angle, the perspective changes the horizontals and verticals into a converging pattern that creates a regular sequence of shapes gradually diminishing in size.

The progression of concentric shapes in **a** establishes a rhythmic pattern. Radiating from the small, black, irregular square in the center, the shapes not only grow larger, but subtly change to become more curvilinear and rounded as the size increases. All the brushstrokes repeat this same rhythmic pattern.

In **b** the rhythmic sequence of shapes moving horizontally across the format is clear whether we look at the white triangles or the black pointed planes. Both shapes progress regularly from narrow to wider and back again in an orderly rhythm.

Example **c** is similar to **a**, but here the increasingly larger circles are arranged in a freer nonconcentric pattern. The rhythmic progression in size, however, is still clear.

a Friedenreich Hundertwasser. *Der Grosse Weg* (The Big Road). 1959. Polyvinyl acetate on canvas, 5′3⅛″ × 5′2⅜″ (1.62 × 1.6 m). Österreichische Galerie, Vienna. © Copyright 1978 by Gruener Janura AG, Glarus/Switzerland. All rights reserved.
b Francis Celentano. *Flowing Phalanx.* 1956. Synthetic polymer paint on canvas, 34⅛″ × 46⅛″ (87 × 117 cm). Museum of Modern Art, New York (Larry Aldrich Foundation Fund).
c Frank Kupka. *Disks of Newton.* 1912. Oil on canvas, 39½″ × 29″ (101 × 74 cm). Philadelphia Museum of Art (Louise and Walter Arensberg Collection).

a

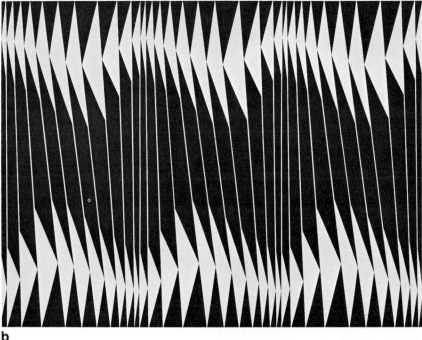

b

c

Line

a

b

Line

Of all the elements in art, line is the most familiar to us. Since most tools that we use for writing and drawing are pointed, we have been making lines constantly since we were young children **(a)**.

What is a line? Other than a mark made by a pointed tool, it is a form that has length and width, but the width is so tiny compared to the length that we perceive line as having only the one dimension. Geometry defines a line as an infinite number of points. The usual art definition of a line is a moving dot. This latter definition is useful to remember, because it recognizes the inherent dynamic quality of line. A line is created by movement. Since our eyes must move to follow it, line's potential to suggest motion is basic. The drawing by Paul Klee **(b)** shows the idea clearly. Klee's line seems to be actually moving before our eyes. The fact that the drawing depicts a head becomes secondary to the dynamic activity of the line.

Line is capable of infinite variety. Example **c** shows just a few of the almost unlimited variations possible under the category *line*. A curious feature of line is its power of suggestion. What an expressive tool it can be for the artist! A line is a minimum statement, made quickly with a minimum of effort but seemingly able to convey all sorts of moods and feelings. The lines pictured in **c** are truly abstract shapes: they depict no objects, and yet we can read into them emotional and expressive qualities. Think of all the adjectives we can apply to lines. We often describe lines as being nervous, angry, happy, free, quiet, excited, calm, graceful, dancing, and so many more qualities. The power of suggestion in this basic element is very great.

a Mark Odom. Untitled drawing.
b Paul Klee. *The Mocker Mocked.* 1930. Oil on canvas, 17 × 20⅝″ (43 × 52 cm). Museum of Modern Art, New York (gift of J. B. Neumann).
c Line has almost unlimited variations.

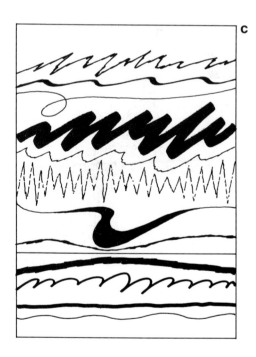

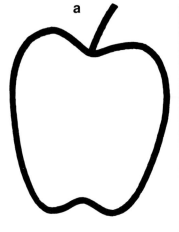

a

b

c

Line

Line is important to the artist because it can describe shape, and by shape we recognize objects. Example **a** is immediately understood as a picture of an apple. It does not have the dimension or mass of an apple; it does not have the color or texture of an apple; it is not the actual size of an apple. Nevertheless, we recognize an apple from the one visual clue of its distinctive shape.

A well-known cliché states that there are no lines in nature. This is perhaps a bit misleading, since there *are* line-like elements in our natural and manufactured environment. Such things as tree twigs, telephone wires, spider webs, railroad tracks, tall grass, and so forth certainly are linear in feeling. What the cliché is addressing is illustrated in **b** and **c**. Example **c** is a line drawing—a drawing of *lines* that are *not* present in the photograph **(b)** or in the original scene. In the photograph, there is of course no black line that runs around each ob-

ject. The lines in the drawing are actually showing *edges,* whereas in the photo areas of different value (or color) meet, showing the end of one object and the beginning of another. Line is therefore an artistic shorthand, useful because, with a comparatively few strokes, an artist can describe and identify the shapes so that we understand the image.

Line drawings, with the lines describing the edges of various forms, abound in art. Example **d** is just one possibility. The German artist George Grosz has taken a complicated social statement—with such diverse elements as figures, buildings, and armaments—and reduced it to a simple but readable statement of line.

a Line describes the shape of a form and helps us identify objects when other characteristics are missing.
b Areas of different value delineate the various objects in this scene.
c Line, as an artistic shorthand, depicts the edges of shapes.
d George Grosz. *The Ruler.* 1925. Brush and black ink on white paper, 21 × 17″ (53 × 42 cm). Private collection.

Line

Line has served the artist as a basic tool ever since cave dwellers drew with a charred stick on the cave walls. *Actual* lines **(a)** may vary greatly in weight, character, or other qualities. There are two other types of line that figure importantly in pictorial composition.

An *implied* line is created by positioning a series of points so that the eye tends automatically to connect them. The "dotted line" is an example familiar to us all **(b)**. Think also of the "line" waiting for a bus, obviously a number of figures standing in a row forming an implied line.

A *psychic* line is illustrated by **c**. Here there is no real line, not even intermittent points, and yet we *feel* a line—a mental connection between the two elements. This usually occurs when something looks or points in a certain direction. Our eyes invariably follow, and a psychic line results.

All three types of line are present in Perugino's painting of the Crucifixion **(d)**. *Actual* lines are clear, for the edges of figures and background objects are clearly delineated. An *implied* line is created at the bottom, where the Virgin's feet, the base of the cross, and St. John's feet form a series of points that connect into a horizontal line **(e)**. This line is picked up in the horizon-

tal shadows of the side panels. *Psychic* lines occur as our eyes follow the direction each figure is looking. St. John looks up at Christ, and Christ gazes down at the Virgin; this gives us a distinct feeling of a central triangle. Both St. Jerome and Mary Magdalene also look at Christ, thus forming a second broader triangle. The purpose of these lines is of course to unify or visually tie together the various elements. Perugino's painting may seem static, perhaps a bit posed and artificial, but it is admirably organized into a clear, coherent pattern.

Artists should always anticipate the movement of the viewer's eye around their compositions. They can to a large extent control this movement, and the various types of lines can be a valuable tool.

a There are many types of actual lines, each varying in weight and character.
b The points in an implied line are automatically connected by the eye.
c When one object points to another, the eye connects the two in a psychic line.
d Pietro Perugino. *Crucifixion with Saints.* Before 1481. Panel transferred to canvas; center, 40 × 22¼" (102 × 57 cm), laterals each 37½ × 12" (95 × 30 cm). National Gallery of Art, Washington, D.C. (Andrew Mellon Collection).
e Actual, implied, and psychic lines all are present in *Crucifixion with Saints* **(d)**.

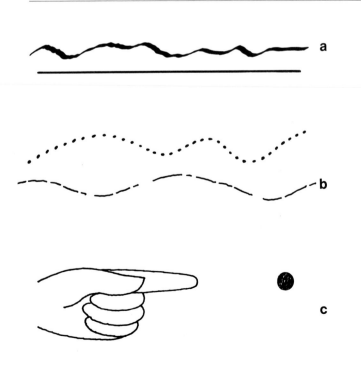

d

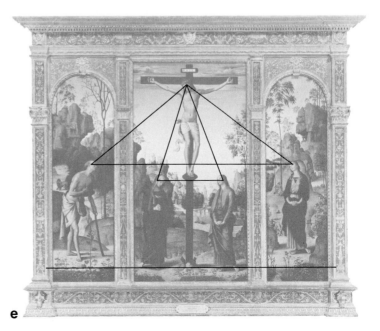

e

Line

Line Direction

There is one important characteristic of line that should be remembered—its direction. A horizontal line implies quiet and repose, probably because we associate a horizontal body posture with rest or sleep. A vertical line, as in a standing body, undoubtedly has more potential of activity. But it is the diagonal line that most suggests motion. In so many of the active movements of life (skiing, running, swinging, skating) the body is leaning, so we automatically see diagonals as movement. There is no doubt that we imply more action, more dynamic momentum, from **b** than from **a**. Example **a** is a static, calm pattern; **b** is exciting and changing.

One other factor is involved in this quality of direction. There are occasional round or oval paintings, but the vast majority of works are rectangular in shape. Therefore, any horizontal or vertical line within the painting is parallel to, and repetitious of, an edge of the format. These horizontal and vertical lines within a design are called *stabilizers*—elements that reduce any feeling of movement. The lines in **a** are parallel to the top and bottom; in **b**, none are.

Poussin's painting **(c)** contains predominantly horizontal and vertical lines, the diagonal road

being the major exception. These lines are diagramed in **d**. The emphasis, extending even to the clouds, is not just chance. The artist planned it. This painting often is called a *classical* work—a term that implies a static, serene, unchanging image. The emphasis on horizontals and verticals is a major factor in this classicism.

Matisse' *Decorative Figure* **(e)** is an odd painting in respect to horizontals and verticals. We are accustomed to seeing pictures with figures in action posed against static backgrounds. Matisse has reversed this norm. The nude figure is highly rectilinear, with many horizontal and vertical outlines, and therefore quite immobile. The background, however, fairly dances with diagonal lines and writhing curves in diagonal patterns on the walls and floor.

a Horizontal lines usually imply rest, or lack of motion.
b Diagonal lines usually imply movement and action.
c Nicolas Poussin. *The Funeral of Phocion.* 1648. Oil on canvas, 3′11″ × 5′10½″ (1.19 × 1.79 m). Louvre, Paris.
d The great number of horizontal and vertical lines in *The Funeral of Phocion* **(c)** suggest calmness and serenity.
e Henri Matisse. *Decorative Figure on an Ornamental Background.* 1927. Oil on canvas, c. 4 × 3′ (1.22 × .91 m). Musée National d'Art Moderne, Paris.

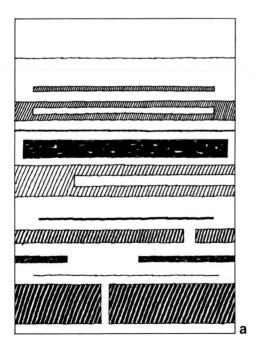

a

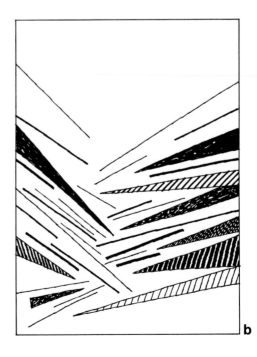

b

c

d

e

Line

Regardless of the chosen medium, when line is the main element of an image, the result is what we call a *drawing*. There are two general types of drawings: *contour* and *gesture*.

When line is used to follow the edges of forms, to describe their outlines, the result is called a *contour* drawing. This is probably the most common use of line in art, and **a** is an example. This portrait by Ingres is a precise drawing with extremely delicate lines carefully describing the features and the folds of the coat. The slightly darker emphasis on the head establishes the focal point. We cannot help but admire the sureness of the drawing, the absolute accuracy of observation.

Rodin's pen-and-ink drawing of a nude **(b)** is also a contour drawing, but this work has a markedly different character. It obviously was done very quickly, and the line moves rapidly and freely around the body's contours. Details are ignored; notice the sketchy quality of the hands and feet. Rodin's pen suggests the voluptuous curves of the body in a spontaneous manner, rather than recording exact details.

The other common type of drawing is called a *gesture* drawing. In this instance describing shapes is less important than showing the action taking place. Line does not stay at the edges, but moves freely within forms. Gesture drawings are not drawings of objects as much as drawings of movement. Because of its very nature, this type of line is almost always drawn quickly and spontaneously. It captures the momentary changing aspect of the subject, rather than recording nuances of form. Van Dyck's *Diana and Endymion* **(c)** is a gesture drawing. Here and there a few contour lines appear, but most lines are concerned with the movement of the swooping figures at the right and the swirl of drapery.

In the drawing by Diziani **(d)** the rapid, almost scribbled ink line builds up the figures starting from the gesture of the poses, rather than beginning with clearly defined edges. The artist suggests swaying trees, but we see no definite foliage shapes.

While quite different approaches to drawing, these two categories are, of course, not mutually exclusive. Many drawings will combine elements of both.

a Jean Auguste Dominique Ingres. *Portrait of a Young Man.* c. 1815. Pencil, 11½ × 8¾″ (29 × 22 cm). Museum Boymans-van Beuningen, Rotterdam.
b Auguste Rodin. *Female Nude.* Late 19th–early 20th century. Pen and ink on tan paper. Private collection.
c Anthony van Dyck. *Diana and Endymion.* 1621–30. Pen and brush, 7½ × 9″ (19 × 23 cm). Pierpont Morgan Library, New York.
d Gaspare Diziani. *The Flight into Egypt.* 1733. Black pencil and pen and sepia on yellowish paper, 11⅝ × 8½″ (30 × 22 cm). Museo Correr, Venice.

Line

Merely to state that a particular artist used line is not very descriptive, because line is capable of infinite variety. The illustrations on these two pages give only a small sampling of the linear possibilities available to the artist. A similar subject matter has been chosen so that differences in linear technique can be emphasized. The line technique chosen in each case is basically responsible for the different effects immediately obvious in the three works.

Example **a** shows a drawing by Ingres. Like many drawings, this was a study for a later painting, the *Grande Odalisque*. Artists often use the relatively easy and quick medium of drawing to try out various compositional possibilities. This drawing is an extremely elegant image. The sinuous flowing curves of the nude are rendered in a delicate, restrained, often an almost disappearing, light line. The actual proportions of the body are altered to stress the long, sweeping, opposing curves that lend the drawing its feeling of quiet grace.

Restraint and understatement are not characteristics of **b**. Rather, the pen-and-ink image of Eve (a detail from Dürer's *Adam and Eve*) is a strong statement. The stark brown background gives a definite emphasis to the body's contour. Dürer then used a series of parallel lines in a criss-cross pattern (called *cross-hatching*) to create some areas of tone, which give a feeling of volume and roundness to the figure.

Example **c**, a drawing by Maillol, also includes some areas of value to suggest volume. However, the black chalk produces a much softer effect than did Dürer's necessarily hard pen strokes. Maillol's image, therefore, is more sensuous, more suggestive of the softness of flesh. The contour lines are definite but smudgy and soft, reinforcing the idea of the bodies' resiliency. The effect is almost an equal emphasis on form and texture.

a Jean Auguste Dominique Ingres. Study for the *Grande Odalisque*. c. 1814. Pencil, 4⅞ × 10½″ (12 × 27 cm). Louvre, Paris.

b Albrecht Dürer. *Adam and Eve*, detail. 1504. Pen and brown ink with wash on white paper, 9⅝ × 8″ (24 × 20 cm). Pierpont Morgan Library, New York.

c Aristide Maillol. *Two Female Nudes*. Early 20th century. Black chalk, heightened with white, 47⅛ × 37″ (121 × 95 cm). Courtesy Gallery Daber, Paris.

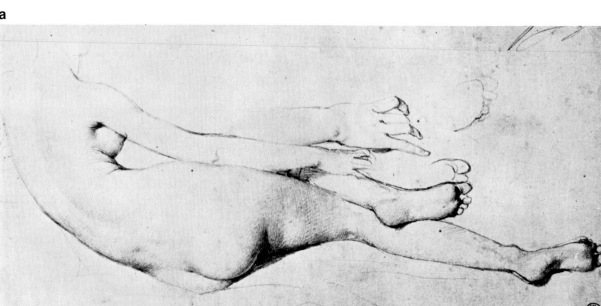

a

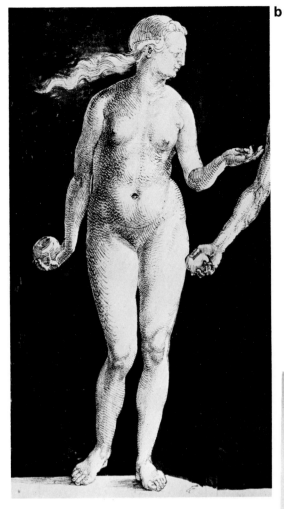

b

c

Line

The female nude by Marquet in **a** is certainly not delicate in either technique or feeling. Here the ink line, done with a brush, is heavy and bold, with variations of thickness. Rather than carefully rendering the body contours, Marquet merely suggests them with a spontaneous, dynamic line moving quickly and somewhat imprecisely around the forms. The gray areas in the background, created with a nearly dry brush, reinforce the spontaneous effect, so that we can almost feel the rapid, scribble-like movement of the brush.

A drawing by Daumier **(b)** has a definite theme beyond portraying a woman: it is titled *Fright*. Notice how the line technique conveys this idea. The whole drawing implies movement; we can feel the woman pulling back, recoiling in fear. There is no one contour line. Many lines of varying weight and character (pencil and charcoal) evoke the forms. The hand, for example, is suggested with a few strokes, not clearly defined. Where the contour does emerge, it is built up of repeated strokes. Some lines are mere gesture lines showing the figure's movement. We sense the artist working rapidly, moving all over the whole drawing at once.

Ballerina by Seurat **(c)** is a unique type of drawing. The line is almost totally confined to the background. The figure is silhouetted against areas of soft, vertical, linear strokes of conté crayon. Only a few lines within the body suggest the bodice straps, hat, and so forth. The effect is a soft, delicate understatement. Contour is vague and indefinite, with only a faint line here and there actually defining an edge, giving the drawing an abstract quality.

It should be obvious that the linear technique you choose can produce emotional or expressive qualities in the final pattern. Solid and bold, quiet and flowing, delicate and dainty, jagged and nervous, or any of countless other possibilities will influence the effect on the viewer of your drawing or design. Choose a theme or decide the effect you wish to impart, and fit the linear technique to it.

a Albert Marquet. *Nude.* c. 1910–12.
Brush (?) and India ink, 11⅝ × 8⅛″ (31 × 22 cm).
National Gallery of Canada, Ottawa.
b Honoré Daumier. *Fright.*
Pencil and charcoal, 8 × 9¼″ (20 × 23 cm).
Art Institute of Chicago (gift of Robert Allison).
c Georges Seurat. *Ballerina.* 1880 or 1884. Conté crayon,
9 × 5¾″ (23 × 15 cm). Private collection, New York.

a

b

c

Line

Line in Painting

Line *can* be an important element in painting. Painting basically deals with areas of color, so its effect is different from that of drawing, which limits the elements involved. Still, line becomes important to painting when the artist purposely chooses to outline forms, as Degas does in **a**. Several figures and the umbrellas have obvious black outlines. Many of the colored areas are so close in value to the sand background that the outlines are needed to give definition to the forms.

Line is obvious in the detail of Venus from Botticelli's famous painting **(b)**. The goddess' hair is a beautiful pattern of flowing, graceful, swirling lines. The hand is delineated from the breast by only the slightest value difference; a delicate dark line clearly outlines the hand.

Compare the use of line in Botticelli's painting with that in **c**. Both works stress the use of line, but the similarity ends with that. *Nurse,* by Lichtenstein **(c)**, employs an extremely heavy, bold line—almost a crude line reminiscent of the drawing in comic books. Each artist has adapted his technique to his theme. Compare the treatment of the hair. Venus is portrayed as the embodiment of all grace and

beauty, her hair a mass of elegant lines in a delicate arabesque pattern. The nurse's hair, by contrast, is a flat, colored area, boldly outlined and with a few slashing, heavy strokes to define its texture. In a comment on American culture, aesthetics and subtlety have been stripped away, leaving a crass, blatantly commercial image.

The use of a black or dark line in a design is often belittled as a "crutch." There is no doubt that a dark, linear structure can often lend some desirable emphasis when the initial color or value pattern seems to provide little excitement. But critics rarely derogate Rouault **(d)**, who made almost a trademark of heavy, black outlines. In this master's hands, the heavy line lent a glowing, luminous quality to the colors.

a Edgar Degas. *Beach Scene (Bains de Mer).* Before 1877. Paper mounted on canvas, 18½ × 32½'' (47 × 83 cm). National Gallery, London (reproduced by courtesy of the Trustees).
b Sandro Botticelli. *The Birth of Venus,* detail. c. 1480. Oil on canvas, 5'8⅞'' × 9⅞'' (1.75 × 2.79 m). Uffizi, Florence.
c Roy Lichtenstein. *Nurse.* 1964. Magna on canvas, 4' (1.22 m) square. Collection Karl Stroher, Darmstadt, West Germany.
d Georges Rouault. *Christ Mocked by Soldiers.* 1932. Oil on canvas, 36¼ × 28½'' (92 × 72 cm). Museum of Modern Art, New York (anonymous gift).

a

b

c

d

Line

Line becomes important in a painting when the contours of the forms are sharply defined and the eye is drawn to the edges. David's painting *The Death of Socrates* **(a)** contains no actual outlines, as we have seen in other examples. However, the contour edges of the many figures are very clearly defined. A clean edge separates each of the elements in the painting, so that a line tracing of these edges would show us the whole scene. The color adds interest, but we are most aware of the essential *drawing* underneath. As a mundane comparison, remember the coloring books we had as children and, as we took out our crayons, the parental warnings to "stay within the lines." The David work would be classified as a "linear" painting despite the absence of actual lines.

A linear painting is distinguished by its clarity. The emphasis on edges, with the resulting separation of forms, makes a clear, definite statement. Even an abstract painting, which simplifies form and ignores details, presents this effect **(b)**.

One other facet of line's role in painting should be noted. Some artists use a linear technique in applying color. The color areas are built up by repeated linear strokes of the brush, which are not smoothed over. Toulouse-Lautrec's café scene **(c)** shows this technique. The artist actually drew with the brush; almost every area is constructed of variously colored linear strokes. Some of these lines are very bold, as in the curtain at the left.

Van Gogh used a similar technique in a more agitated, dynamic way **(d)**. Short, linear strokes swirl around the painting. In both these works the multicolored lines give an interesting textural effect to the various areas and provide another element of visual unity.

a Jacques Louis David. *The Death of Socrates.* 1787. Oil on canvas, 4'3" × 6'5¼" (1.3 × 1.96 m). Metropolitan Museum of Art, New York (Wolfe Fund, 1931).
b Juan Gris. *Guitar and Flowers.* 1912. Oil on canvas, 44⅛ × 27⅝" (112 × 70 cm). Museum of Modern Art, New York (bequest of Anna E. Levene in memory of her husband Dr. Phoebus A. T. Levene).
c Henri de Toulouse-Lautrec. *A La Mie (Last Crumbs).* 1891. Oil on canvas, 19¾ × 27½" (50 × 70 cm). Museum of Fine Arts, Boston (S. A. Denio Fund).
d Vincent van Gogh. *Road with Cypresses.* 1890. Oil on canvas, 36 × 28½" (92 × 73 cm). Rijksmuseum Kröller-Müller, Otterlo, Netherlands.

a

b

c

d

a

b

c

d

Line

David's mythological work **(a)** is termed a linear painting. All the forms are depicted with sharp, clear edges. There is no confusion about where one form ends and another begins. If we traced all these contour edges **(b)**, we would have a line drawing that presents the whole scene. The color and value variations add a feeling of volume and visual interest, but the line version is perfectly understandable.

The effect is quite different in **c**. This painting by de la Tour puts more emphasis on color and value than on line. In each of the figures only part of the body is revealed by a sharp contour, but the edge then disappears into a mysterious darkness. This is termed *lost-and-found* contour: now you see it, now you don't. The artist gives us a few clues, and we fill in the rest. For example, when we see a sharply defined hand, we will automatically assume an arm is there, although we do not see it. A line interpretation of this painting **(d)** proves that we do not get a complete scene. Bits and pieces float confusingly, and we cannot understand the image at all.

Example **e** is a rather extreme version of lost-and-found contour. The group of people gathered to watch the experiment are illuminated only by the very dim light coming from the scientific apparatus. Bits of highlight here and there pick out faces, but most of the figures disappear in the darkness.

A strong linear contour structure in a painting provides clarity. Lost-and-found contour gives only relative clarity, for many forms are not fully described. However, it results in a much more exciting, emotional image.

a Jacques Louis David. *Mars Disarmed by Venus and the Graces.* 1824. Oil on canvas, 9'10" × 8'7" (3 × 2.62 m). Musée Royal des Beaux-Arts, Brussels.
b The outlines of the forms in *Mars Disarmed* **(a)** are so clear that a line drawing of it is perfectly understandable.
c Georges de la Tour. *St. Sebastian Mourned by St. Irene and Her Ladies.* 1649. Oil on canvas. Staatliche Museen, West Berlin.
d A line drawing of *St. Sebastian* **(c)** is confusing, because the shapes are defined by changing light and shadow, not by line.
e Joseph Wright of Derby. *Experiment with the Air Pump.* 1768. Oil on canvas, 6½" × 8' (1.84 × 2.44 m). Tate Gallery, London.

e

Shape / Form

Shape/Form Introduction

A *shape* is a visually perceived area created either by an enclosing line or by color and value changes defining the outer edges. A shape can also be called a *form*. The two terms are generally synonymous and often are used interchangeably. Shape is a more precise term, because form does have other meanings in art. For example, *form* may be used in a broad sense to describe the total visual organization of a work. A work's "artistic form" refers not just to shape, but also to color, texture, value pattern, composition, balance, and so forth. Thus, to avoid confusion, the term *shape* is more specific.

Shape usually is considered a two-dimensional element, with the words *volume* or *mass* applied to the three-dimensional equivalent. In simplest terms, paintings have shapes, and sculptures have masses.

Design, or composition, is basically the arrangement of shapes. Chardin's still life **(a)** is in effect an arrangement of various circular shapes. Of course, the color, texture, and value of these shapes are important, but the basic element is shape. Historically, line's most important role in art has been in delineating shape. Pictures certainly exist without color, without any significant textural interest, and even without line—but rarely without shape. Only the fuzziest, most diffuse of Impressionism's shimmering images of light **(b)** can be said virtually to dispense with shape.

In designing your own patterns and looking at those of others, you must develop the ability to look beyond interesting subject matter to the basic element of shape. A circle in a painting or design may literally represent an orange, a shield, a breast, a balloon, a wheel, the sun, an angel's halo, or countless other round items. However, its importance in pictorial composition is as a *shape*—a circle. In design, seeing shapes is primary; reading their meaning is interesting, but secondary.

Example **c** is a picture created by a computer. It makes an interesting image, because it is clearly a pattern of some 250 squares of various grays *and,* incidentally, is a picture of Abraham Lincoln. Here a mid-point has been established at which we are aware equally of the basic design shapes and the subject matter. Several images were tested to find this very point, where most people could indeed see both qualities. When more, smaller squares were used, people saw only Lincoln; with fewer, larger squares, they saw only the gray shapes and no subject matter of Lincoln's head.

a Jean Baptiste Siméon Chardin. *Still Life with A White Mug.* c. 1756. Oil on canvas, 13 × 16¼″ (33 × 41 cm). National Gallery of Art, Washington, D.C. (gift of W. Averell Harriman Foundation in memory of Marie N. Harriman).
b Claude Monet. *Morning Haze.* c. 1892. Oil on canvas, 29⅛ × 36⅝″ (74 × 93 cm). National Gallery of Art, Washington, D.C. (Chester Dale Collection, 1958).
c Spatially quantized image of Abraham Lincoln. Blocpix® image. Courtesy E. T. Manning.

a

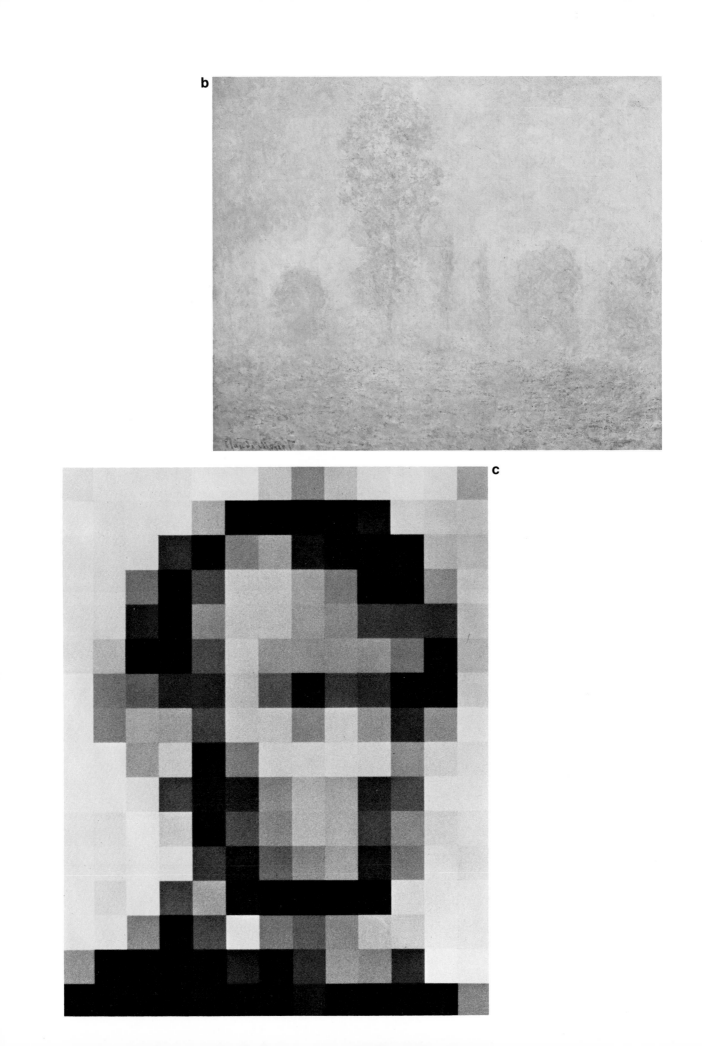

b

c

Shape/Form

The shapes in Eakins' portrait **(a)** would be described as *naturalistic*. Here the artist has skillfully reproduced the visual image, the forms and proportions seen in nature, with an illusion of volume and three-dimensional space. Naturalism is what most people call "realism," meaning of course *visual* realism. The radically different visual effect of a similar subject in Soutine's painting **(b)** results from this artist's use of *distortion*. In using distortion, the artist disregards the shapes and forms of nature, purposely changing or exaggerating them. Sometimes distortion is meant to provoke an emotional response on the part of the viewer; sometimes it serves merely to emphasize the design elements inherent in the subject matter.

Many people think that distortion is a 20th-century development. Now that the camera can easily and cheaply reproduce the appearance of the world around us—a role formerly filled by painting—distortion, or the degree of distortion, has greatly increased in 20th-century art. However, distortion has always been a facet of art; the artist has rarely been just a human camera.

Distortion of the figures is evident in the 11th-century illumination shown in **c**. We can identify distortion of size, of human proportions, and of anatomically possible positions. But in **d** the contemporary artist Willem de Kooning uses even greater distortion of the shapes and proportions of a woman. The leering face with its huge eyes and enlarged "lipsticked" smile, the enormous breasts, and the dainty feet all emerging from the dynamic swirl of paint show a purposeful disregard of the natural image.

a Thomas Eakins. *Miss Van Buren.* 1889–91. Oil on canvas, 45 × 32″ (110 × 81 cm). Phillips Collection, Washington, D.C.
b Chaim Soutine. *Woman in Red.* c. 1922. Oil on canvas, 25 × 21″ (64 × 53 cm). Musée d'Art Moderne de la Ville de Paris.
c *Annunciation to the Shepherds,* from the Gospel lectionary of Henry II. c. 1002–24. Illumination, 13 × 9⅜″ (33 × 24 cm). Bayerische Staatsbibliothek, Munich.
d Willem de Kooning. *Woman and Bicycle.* 1952–53. Oil on canvas, 6′4½″ × 4′1″ (1.94 × 1.24 m). Whitney Museum of American Art, New York.

a

b

c

d

Shape/Form

Naturalism is concerned with *appearance*. It gives the true-to-life, honest appearance of shapes in the world around us. In contrast, there is a specific type of artistic distortion called *idealism*. Idealism reproduces the world not as it is, but as it *should be*. Nature is improved upon. All the flaws, accidents, and incongruities of the visual world are corrected.

Caravaggio's *The Entombment* **(a)** is naturalistic. The figures look natural, like people we see every day. Even Christ is not unduly handsome or godlike. However, in Raphael's painting **(b)** the form exemplifies *idealism*. The utterly graceful, elegant, beautiful figures could not exist. They represent a purely conceptual image of perfection that nature does not produce.

Idealism is a recurrent theme in art, as it is in civilized society. We are all idealistic; we all strive for perfection. Despite overwhelming his-

torical evidence, we continue to believe we can create a world without war, poverty, sickness, or social injustice. Obviously, art will periodically reflect this dream of a utopia. The Greek Hellenic period of the 5th century B.C. produced images that established standards of visual perfection for many succeeding generations. The statue in **c** was a conscious attempt to discover the ideal proportions for the human body. This sculpture was not modeled after any human figure. It represented a visual paragon that cannot be found in nature.

a Caravaggio. *The Entombment.* 1602–03.
 Oil on canvas, 12′ × 6′9″ (3.66 × 2.06 m). Vatican, Rome.
b Raphael. *The Alba Madonna.* c. 1511. Oil on panel transferred to canvas, diameter 37¼″ (95 cm). National Gallery of Art, Washington, D.C. (Andrew Mellon Collection, 1937).
c Polyclitus. *Spear Carrier.* Roman copy of Greek original of c. 450–440 B.C.
 Marble, height 6′6″ (1.98 m). Museo Nazionale, Naples.

a

b

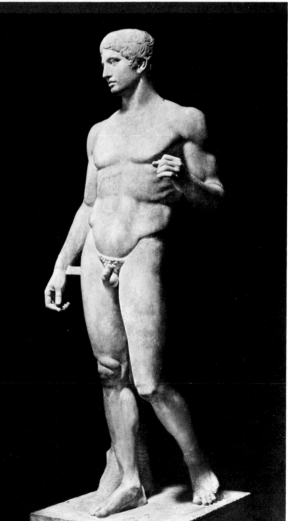

c

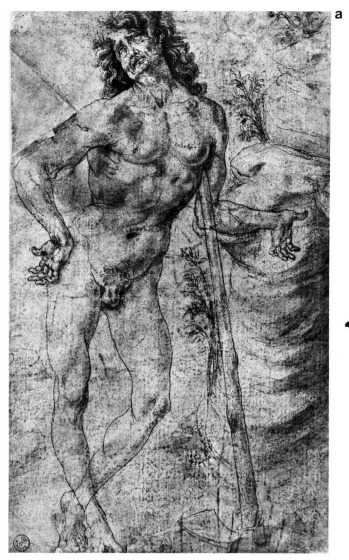

a

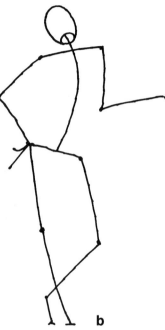

b

c

Shape/Form

Abstraction

A specific kind of artistic distortion is called *abstraction*. Abstraction implies a simplification of natural shapes to their essential, basic character. Details are ignored as the shapes are reduced to their simplest terms. The stick figure that we all drew as children is a familiar (and extreme) example of abstraction. The Renaissance drawing of a man in **a** is *naturalistic* in recording all the complicated shapes comprising the human body. Example **b** describes the same pose in the simplest way, ignoring every detail and reducing complex shapes to the few lines that define the figure's stance. These simple lines comprise the *essence* of the complicated structure in **a**.

Since no artist, no matter how skilled or careful, can possibly reproduce *every* detail of the natural scene, any painting could be called an abstraction. But the term most often is applied to works in which this simplification is visually obvious and is important to the final pictorial effect. Of course, the degree of abstraction can vary. In Seurat's painting **(c)** the figures are abstracted to some extent. Many details have been omitted in reducing the figures to simple, strong, rather flat shapes. Still, the subject matter is immediately recognizable, and we are not too far from the naturalistic image. When the degree of abstraction is fairly slight, as in this example, we often consider the shapes to be *generalized* or *stylized*.

In **d** the amount of abstraction is much greater. This poster for the play *Equus* clearly illustrates a horse's head, but the head has been highly simplified into a flat pattern of triangles, circles, and rectangles. The horse's mane has become a series of parallel lines, and even the teeth are simple squares. This design illustrates a widely accepted principle: All form, however complex, is essentially based on, and can be reduced to, a few geometric shapes.

The communication of ideas by images instead of words is valuable in international events, where participants speak many languages. The directional signs in **e** designated service areas at EXPO 67 in Montréal. In each case, the pictorial idea has been reduced and abstracted to a simple black-and-white symbol.

a Antonio del Pollaiuolo. Study of *Adam*. Pen over black chalk with wash, 11 × 7¼″ (28 × 18 cm). Uffizi, Florence.
b An abstraction of the study of *Adam* **(a)** reveals its basic structure.
c Georges Seurat. *A Sunday Afternoon on the Island of La Grande Jatte.* 1884–86. Oil, 6′9¼″ × 10′1¼″ (2.06 × 3.05 m). Art Institute of Chicago (Helen Birch Bartlett Memorial Collection).
d Poster for the play *Equus.* 1976. Gilbert Lesser, designer.
e *First Aid* and *Post Office* signs for EXPO 67, Montréal. Harry Boller, designer. Courtesy GRAPHIS magazine, Zurich.

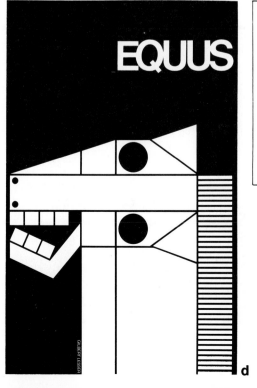

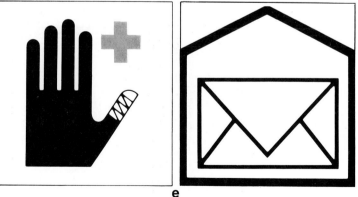

Shape / Form

According to common usage, the term *abstraction* might be applied to the painting in **a**. This is misleading, however, because the shapes in this work are not natural forms that have been artistically simplified. They do not represent anything other than the geometric forms we see. Rather, they are pure form. A better term, then, to describe these shapes is *nonobjective*—that is, shapes with absolutely no object reference, no subject-matter suggestion.

Most of the original design drawings in this book are nonobjective patterns. Often, it is easier to see an artistic principle or element without a distracting veneer of subject matter. In a similar way, artists in this century are forcing us to observe their works as visual patterns, not storytelling narratives. Without a story, subject, or even definable shapes, the painting must be appreciated solely as a visual design.

Lack of subject matter does not necessarily rule out emotional content to the image. Some nonobjective works are cool, aloof, and unemotional. Paintings such as the one in **b** present purely nonobjective, geometric shapes that are, as Plato said, "free from the sting of desire." Example **c** is equally nonobjective, but here the result is highly emotional. The thick paint in agitated, fluid brush strokes gives us a dynamic pattern. This spontaneous, restless gesture painting is an exciting creation in pigment.

a Kasimir Malevich. *Suprematist Composition: Airplane Flying.* 1914. Oil on canvas, 22⅞ × 19″ (58 × 48 cm). Museum of Modern Art, New York (purchase).
b László Moholy-Nagy. *A II.* 1924. Oil on canvas, 3′9⅝″ × 4′5⅝″ (1.16 × 1.36 m). Solomon R. Guggenheim Museum, New York.
c Willem de Kooning. *Park Rosenberg.* 1957. Oil on canvas, 6′8″ × 5′10½″ (2.03 × 1.79 m). Collection Mr. and Mrs. I. Donald Grossman, New York.

a

b

c

Shape/Form

Dots

A *dot* is a shape, although generally a very small one. The scale, however, is relative. What might be a "dot" in a large painting could be quite a large shape in a smaller drawing or print. It would be difficult to differentiate absolutely which of the shapes in **a** would qualify as a *dot* and which would not. As **a** illustrates, a dot can function in a design in three ways: (1) as a shape in itself; (2) in a sequential pattern that causes the eye to connect the points and create an implied line (a "dotted line"); (3) massed together to create a larger shape—a shape that by its nature forms a gray value with interesting visual texture.

Dots can be used either to create descriptive shapes or as pure design elements. The French artist Georges Seurat employed a technique often called *pointillism,* in which the paint was applied in small dots of various colors **(b)**. A detail from one of his paintings **(c)** shows how the dots are combined to build up recognizable forms. The painted dots give a unique overall texture to the surface, but the subject matter, while abstracted, is still clear.

a Dots can be used as individual design elements or as a part of larger shapes.
b Georges Seurat. *The Channel at Gravelines, Petit Fort Philippe.* 1890. Oil on canvas, 20 × 36¾″ (74 × 93 cm). Indianapolis Museum of Art (gift of Mrs. James W. Fesler in memory of Daniel W. and Elizabeth C. Marmon).
c Detail of Seurat's *The Channel at Gravelines* **(b).**

a

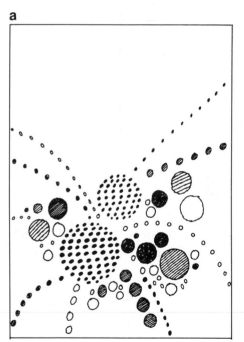

b

c

Shape/Form

It should be recognized that most of the pictures we see reproduced in newspapers, magazines, and books are in reality collections of dots. Any black-and-white "halftone" (a picture with gradations of value) must be reproduced by photographing it through a *screen* or grid. The screen translates the image into black dots of different concentrations; when combined with the white paper, these dots give the visual effect of various grays. The enlargement of a halftone in **a** shows that there is indeed no gray, but a pattern of tiny black dots.

The American painter Larry Poons uses dots just as dots **(b)**. He designs his paintings as compositions of "dots" in various colors and values. Here the dots have no meaning or subject matter. In the same way, Jiří Kolář treats

dots simply as nonobjective elements. The tiny dots create an intricate pattern of lines **(c)**.

When we look closely at the Smithsonian Institution poster in **d**, the design that seems at first to be composed of dots becomes, in reality, a collection of innumerable tiny photographs of faces.

a Enlarged detail of newspaper halftone.
b Larry Poons. *Away Out on the Mountain.* 1965. Acrylic on canvas, 6′ × 12′ (1.83 × 3.05 m). Allen Art Museum, Oberlin, Ohio.
c Jiří Kolář. *Blind Man's Poem.* 1962. Pierced paper, 39⅜ × 27½″ (100 × 70 cm). Galerie Schoeller, Düsseldorf, West Germany.
d *A Nation of Nations.* Poster designed for Smithsonian Institution. 1976. Ivan Chermayeff and Stephan Geissbuhler, Chermayeff & Geismar Associates, designers. Offset lithograph, 39 × 25¾″ (100 × 65 cm).

a

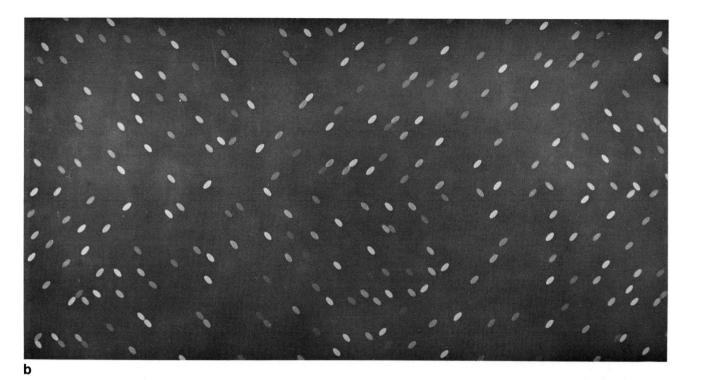

b

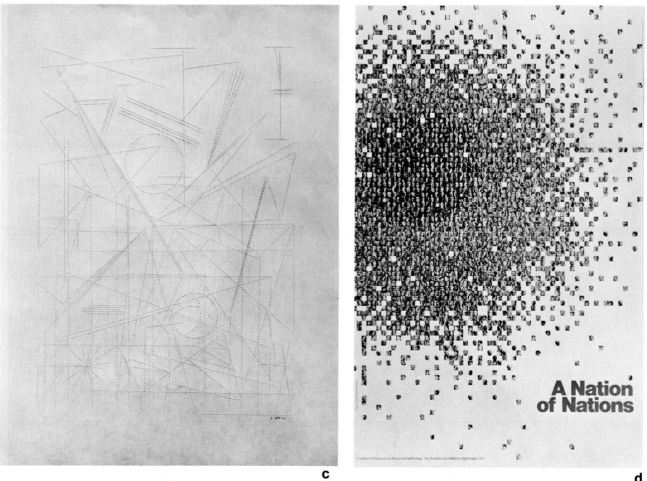

c

d

a

Shape/Form

If we consider only subject matter, **a** and **b** are practically identical. Both are pictures of a violin placed on a table with a sheet of music. But as visual patterns the two are radically different. Part of this difference is one of color, some results from varied placement. But the main contrast stems from the emphasis on different types of shapes.

The painting by Juan Gris **(a)** is a rigid, controlled pattern of what we call *rectilinear* shapes. The shapes are generally geometric in feeling, with hard, straight edges and angular corners. The curves of the violin create a focal point, but most shapes repeat the rectangles of the table and the wall paneling. As a result, the feeling is ordered and static. On the other hand, the Dufy painting **(b)** has an informal, relaxed feeling. This composition emphasizes *curvilinear* shapes. Here the curves of the violin are repeated in the convoluted, twisting Rococo table. Nearly all forms are curved and irregular, flowing along with the artist's rapid brushstrokes to produce a dynamic pattern.

Rectilinear shapes are usually precise, so they are often called artificial or geometric in character. The softer, flowing effect of curvilinear shapes suggests the forms found in nature, hence the alternate terms of *natural* or *biomorphic*. Of course, these are very broad conclusions. In fact, geometric shapes abound in nature, especially in the microscopic structure of elements, and people design many objects with irregular, free-form shapes.

The Gris painting **(a)** illustrates a common design practice. In combining rectilinear and curvilinear shapes, a successful device is to stress one type of shape and use the other sparingly as a point of emphasis. This achieves both an immediate overall unity and a focal point.

a Juan Gris. *The Violin*. 1916. Oil on wood panel, 45½ × 28½" (117 × 73 cm). Kunstmuseum, Basel.
b Raoul Dufy. *The Yellow Violin*. 1949. Oil on canvas, 39½ × 32" (100 × 81 cm). Art Gallery of Ontario, Toronto (gift of Sam and Ayala Zacks, 1970).

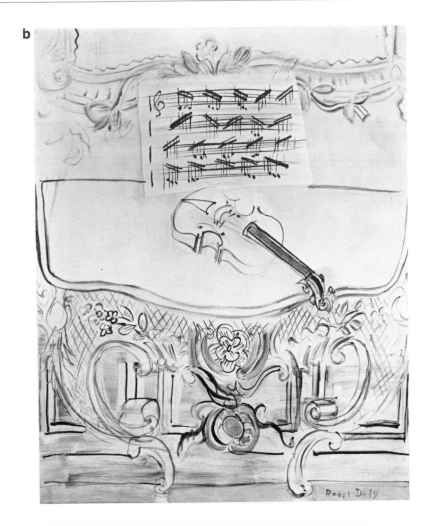

b

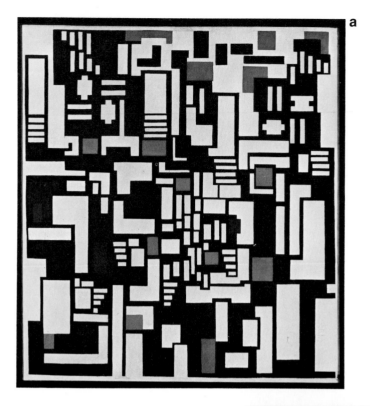

a

b

Shape/Form

The title of the painting by Theo van Doesburg **(a)** describes a theme of card players. However, the forms are so highly abstracted that the subject matter becomes relatively unimportant. What we see is a busy pattern composed of purely rectilinear shapes. Innumerable geometric shapes in a very bold value pattern of light and dark give us a feeling of almost mathematical precision.

Aubrey Beardsley's drawing in **b** shows an equal emphasis on the opposite effect—curvilinear shapes. This drawing is a product of a late-19th-century style called *Art Nouveau*, which put total pictorial emphasis on natural shapes. The languid poses, the flowing drapery, the decorative accessories, even the lavish wigs all provide an incredibly intricate pattern of curvilinear shapes. Every inch of the pattern twists,

twines, and turns to create a restless arabesque of shapes.

Miró's painting in **c** combines the two types of shapes. The artist has emphasized the floating dark curvilinear shapes, but the background is divided into soft, slightly diffused rectangular forms, as a contrast.

a Theo van Doesburg. *Composition IX, Opus 18 (Card Players)*. 1917. Oil on canvas, 45¼ × 41⅜″ (116 × 106 cm). Gemeentemuseum, The Hague.
b Aubrey Beardsley. *The Cave of Spleen.* Drawing for *The Rape of the Lock,* by Alexander Pope, published by Leonard Smithers, London, 1896. Pen and ink, 9⅞ × 6⅛″ (25 × 17 cm). Museum of Fine Arts, Boston.
c Joan Miró. *Painting.* 1933. Oil on canvas, 5′8½″ × 6′5¼″ (1.74 × 1.96 m). Museum of Modern Art, New York (gift of the Advisory Committee).

c

Shape / Form

The four examples in **a** illustrate an important design consideration that is sometimes overlooked. In each of these patterns the black shape is identical. The very different visual effects are caused solely by its placement within the format. This is because the location of the black shape immediately organizes the empty space into various shapes. We refer to these as *positive* and *negative* shapes. The black shape is a positive element, the white empty space the negative shape or shapes. *Figure* and *ground* are other terms used to describe the same idea—the black shape being the figure.

In paintings with subject matter, the idea of object and background is *almost* taken for granted. A portrait by Holbein **(b)** gives an example of the division into positive and negative shapes. It is important to remember that *both* elements have been thoughtfully designed by the artist. The subject is the focal point, but the negative areas created are equally important in the final pictorial effect.

Japanese art intrigues the Western eye because of its unusual design of negative space. Compare the placement of the figure in **b** with that in **c**. In the Japanese print **(c)** the diagonal pose with the decidedly off-center location of the courtesan's head and low placement of the bosom is unexpected. The negative shapes thus created are much more varied and interesting than the rather symmetrical background shapes in the Holbein **(b)**, which lend this painting its air of quiet formality.

a The location of shapes in space organizes that space into positive and negative areas.
b Hans Holbein the Younger. *Anne of Cleves.* 1539. Parchment mounted on canvas, 25⅝ × 18⅞″ (65 × 48 cm). Louvre, Paris.
c Kitagawa Utamaro. *Courtesan,* from the series *Five Varieties of Residents of the Yoshiwara.* c. 1789. Color woodcut, 14¾ × 9⅞″ (37 × 25 cm). Collection Mr. and Mrs. Edwin Grabhorn, San Francisco.

a

b

c

Shape / Form

Integration

Design themes and purposes vary, but generally some sort of integration between the positive and negative shapes is thought desirable. In **a** the shapes and their placement are interesting enough, but they seem to float aimlessly within the format. They also have what we call a "pasted-on" look, since there is little back-and-forth visual movement between the positive shapes and the negative white background. An unrelieved silhouetting of every shape is usually not the most interesting spatial solution. Example **b** has the same shapes in the same positions, but breaking up the "background" into areas of value lends interest as well as better positive/negative integration. The division into positive and negative is flexible.

This integration of positive and negative shapes is so prevalent in art that innumerable works exhibit it. The most common device is to repeat a color in both positive and negative areas, thus giving them a visual link. The artist can also deliberately plan points where the eye will move from object to background. In Botticelli's portrait **(c)** much of the figure is shown in silhouette. However, the darker window frame not only breaks up the background into interesting areas but provides several places where the figure and background are quite close in value, so that the eye moves easily from one to the other.

The background in the painting by Matisse **(d)** is broken up into rather arbitrary areas of light and dark. These negative areas line up with, and continue edges of, the positive shapes, but at the same time they contribute a visual variety: the positive elements are sometimes dark against light and at other times light against dark. Matisse' composition is a more sophisticated version of the effect created in **b**, and again the integration of the shapes is achieved.

a When positive and negative spaces are too rigidly defined, the result is rather uninteresting.
b If the negative areas are made more interesting, the positive/negative integration improves.
c Sandro Botticelli. *Portrait of a Young Man.* c. 1480. Panel, 23 × 15½″ (58 × 39 cm). Collection of the late Sir Thomas Merton, Berkshire, England.
d Henri Matisse. *The Painter and His Model.* 1917. Oil on canvas, 4′9⅜″ × 3′1⅛″ (1.47 × .97 m). Musée National d'Art Moderne, Paris.

a

b

c

d

Shape / Form

Confusion

Sometimes positive and negative shapes are not merely integrated, but integrated to such an extent that there is truly no visual distinction. When we look at the painting in **a**, we automatically see some black shapes on a background. But when we read the artist's title, *White Forms,* suddenly the view changes, and we begin to focus on the *white* shapes, with the black areas now perceived as negative space. The artist has purposely made the positive/negative relationship ambiguous.

In most paintings of the past the separation of object and background was easily seen, even if selected areas visually merged together. However, several 20th-century art styles literally do away with the distinction. The eye can no longer distinguish which shapes are positive and which negative. Or, indeed, perhaps the *whole* area now consists of positive shapes.

Futurism was an early-20th-century style that attempted to portray the moving, dynamic aspects of our modern world. Example **b**, a painting by the Futurist artist Gino Severini, is a pictorial expression of the constantly moving, shifting visual patterns seen in a Parisian nightclub. The surface of the painting shatters into fragmented images of the scene, suggesting constant movement and change. In the process,

any sense of a background of negative shapes is lost, which perhaps is the artist's intent.

Cubism was a movement concerned primarily with the element of shape, but again little distinction was made between the positive and negative. Picasso's portrait in **c** presents abstracted fragments of the subject's face and figure in a pattern that does not let us separate the figure from the background.

The works of M. C. Escher show this same intentional confusion of positive and negative shapes. With great imagination and brilliant technical facility, Escher creates designs that challenge the whole concept of a distinction between the two types of shape. Example **d** is one of many in which Escher literally abolishes negative space. No matter which color value we focus on in this remarkable design, the shapes appear as positive elements.

a Franz Kline. *White Forms.* 1955. Oil on canvas, 6'2⅜" × 4'2¼" (1.89 × 1.28 m). Museum of Modern Art, New York (gift of Philip Johnson).
b Gino Severini. *Dynamic Hieroglyphic of the Bal Tabarin.* 1912. Oil on canvas, with sequins; 5'3⅜" × 5'1½" (1.62 × 1.56 m). Museum of Modern Art, New York (acquired through the Lillie P. Bliss Bequest).
c Pablo Picasso. *Daniel-Henry Kahnweiler.* 1910. Oil on canvas, 39⅝" × 28⅝" (101 × 73 cm). Art Institute of Chicago (gift of Mrs. Gilbert W. Chapman).
d M. C. Escher. *Study of Regular Division of the Plane with Horsemen.* 1946. India ink and watercolor, 12 × 9" (30 × 23 cm). Escher Foundation, Gemeentemuseum, The Hague.

d

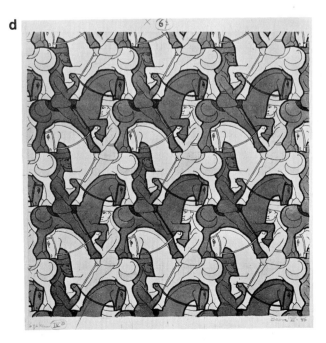

Texture

10

a

Texture

Texture refers to the surface quality of objects. Texture appeals to our sense of touch. Even when we do not actually feel an object, our memory provides the sensory reaction or sensation of touch. In effect, the various light and dark patterns of different textures give visual clues for us to enjoy the textures vicariously. Of course, all objects have some surface quality even if it is only an unrelieved smooth flatness. The element of texture is illustrated in art when an artist has purposely exploited contrasts in surface to provide visual interest.

Many art forms have a basic concern with texture and its visual effects. Architecture today, with contrasts of brick, glass, wood, steel, and concrete, often relies on textural changes for visual excitement. Applied surface decoration has become less important; more emphasis is placed on the honest look and "feel" of the materials themselves. In most of the craft areas texture is an important consideration. Weaving and the textile arts **(a)**, ceramics, jewelry, and

furniture design often rely heavily on the texture of the materials themselves to enhance the design effect.

In sculpture exhibits the "Do Not Touch" signs are a practical (if unhappy) necessity, for so many sculptures appeal to our enjoyment of texture **(b)**. The smooth translucence of marble, the rough grain of wood, the polished or patinated bronze, the irregular drip of molten solder—each adds a distinctive textural quality.

Visual distance can be a factor in texture. Many surfaces from a distance appear relatively smooth. The closer we get, the rougher and more varied the surface becomes, with microscopic photographs even revealing textural patterns invisible to the naked eye.

a Grau-Garriga. *Vestal.* 1972. Tapestry of cotton, wool, and synthetics; 5'8" × 2'2" (1.7 × .65 m). Courtesy Arras Gallery, New York.
b Nobuo Sekine. *Phases of Nothingness—Cone.* 1972. Black granite, height 11¾" (30 cm). Courtesy Tokyo Gallery.

b

Texture

Tactile Texture

There are two categories of artistic texture. Architecture and sculpture employing actual materials have what is called *tactile* texture—texture that can actually be felt. In painting the term tactile texture describes an uneven paint surface, when an artist uses thick pigment (a technique called *impasto*) so that a rough, three-dimensional paint surface results.

As the need and desire for illusionism in art faded, tactile texture became a more common aspect of painting. Paintings now could look like what they truly were—paint on canvas. Modifying the painting's surface became another option available to the artist. Van Gogh was an early exponent of the actual application of paint as a further expressive element. The detail in **a** shows how short brushstrokes of thick, undiluted paint are used to build up the agitated, swirling patterns of his landscapes. The ridges and raised edges of the paint strokes are obvious to the eye.

The visual movement of painted strokes, often applied with a palette knife or very large brushes, was an important aspect of many

Abstract Expressionist paintings. This technique resembled Van Gogh's, but the result was even more dynamic because of the more spontaneous irregular strokes made by the artist. The tactile surface of a Van Gogh can seem almost controlled and regular when compared to that of a de Kooning **(b)**.

At times artists will even mix paint with other materials to add further tactile variety to the surface of the painting. The Spanish artist Antoni Tapies often combined thick pigment with plaster. Example **c** shows his *Great Painting*, a work of somber color but extremely rich tactile surface achieved partly by his mixing sand with the paint.

a Vincent van Gogh. *Road with Cypresses*, detail. 1890.
Oil on canvas, entire work 36 × 28½″ (92 × 73 cm).
Rijksmuseum Kröller-Müller, Otterlo, Netherlands.
b Willem de Kooning. *Woman, Sag Harbor*, detail. 1964.
Oil on wood panel, entire work 6′8″ × 3′ (2.03 × .91 m).
Hirshhorn Museum and Sculpture Garden,
Smithsonian Institution, Washington, D.C.
c Antoni Tapies. *Great Painting*. 1958.
Oil and sand on canvas, 6′7″ × 8′6⅝″ (2.01 × 2.61 m).
Solomon R. Guggenheim Museum, New York.

a

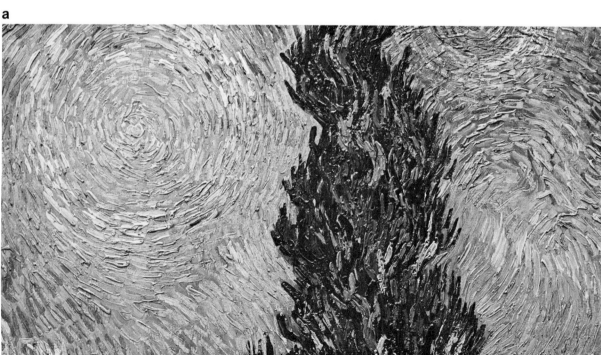

c

b

Texture

Tactile Texture

Collage

Creating a design by pasting down bits and pieces of colored and textured papers, cloth, or other materials is called *collage*. This is an artistic technique that has been popular for centuries, but mainly in the area of folk art. It is really only in the 20th century that collage has been seriously considered a legitimate medium for the fine arts.

The collage method is a very serviceable one. It saves the artist the painstaking, often tedious task of carefully reproducing textures in paint. Collage is an excellent medium for beginners. Forms can be altered or reshaped quickly and easily with scissors. Also, compositional arrangements can more easily be tested (before pasting) than when the design is indelibly rendered in paint.

The German artist Kurt Schwitters worked almost exclusively in collage. His *From Kate Steinitz* **(a)** is an arrangement of castoff scraps of colored and textured papers with some areas of printed type creating further visual texture. In some places the paper is wrinkled purposely to add greater surface interest.

Anne Ryan, an American, worked mainly in collages of cloth. Her *Oval* **(b)** shows the various bits of cloth of contrasting weaves and textures interspersed with bits of various papers. The value differences being so subtle, we concentrate on the tactile textures.

Arthur Dove created a textural relief pattern out of ordinary, everyday objects **(c)**. The interesting arrangement of diagonals and curves is composed of pieces of fishing poles and scraps of denim shirts.

a Kurt Schwitters. *From Kate Steinitz.* 1945. Collage, 13¼ × 10¼″ (33 × 26 cm). Courtesy Marlborough Gallery, Inc., New York.
b Anne Ryan. *Oval.* Collage on paper, 6¾ × 5⅛″ (16 × 12 cm). Collection Mr. and Mrs. John de Menil.
c Arthur Dove. *Goin' Fishin'.* 1925. Collage, 19½ × 24″ (50 × 61 cm). Phillips Collection, Washington, D.C.

a

b

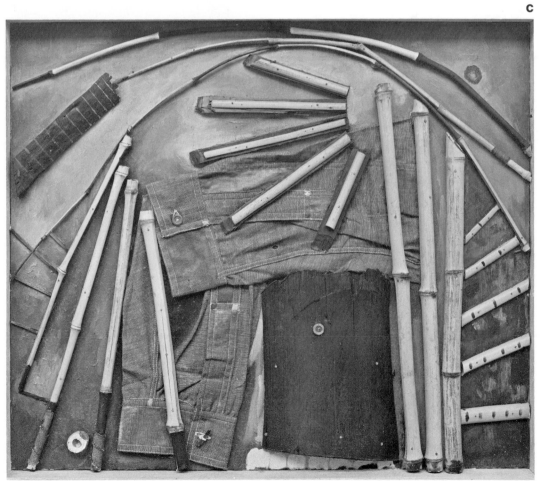

c

Texture

In painting, artists can create the impression of texture on a flat, smooth paint surface. By reproducing the color and value patterns of familiar textures, they can encourage us to see textures where none actually exist. This is called *visual* texture. The impression of texture is purely visual; it cannot be felt or enjoyed by touch, only suggested to our eyes.

One of the pleasures of still-life paintings is the contrast of visual textures. These works, lacking story or emotional content, can be purely visual delights as the artist plays off one simulated texture against another. Still-life painting was extremely popular in 17th-century Flemish art, and countless beautiful examples were created. Example **a**, by de Heem, employs superb textural contrasts: the metallic cup, the crusty bread, the shiny glass, the fuzzy peaches, the transluscent grapes, even the tiny

velvety butterflies. Everyplace we look we encounter a new visual texture.

Today our interest in portraits, such as the one by Van Dyck in **b**, lies not so much in the sitter but in the rendition of the visual textures. The artist has so skillfully suggested the sheen of the satin sleeves, the delicate lace collar, the incredibly fluffy feather fan, and much more. Often, when looking very closely at such a picture, we discover that the texture is not minutely rendered. Instead, the artist has given us a few brushstrokes that from a certain distance perfectly suggest the desired texture.

a Jan Davidsz. de Heem. *Still Life with a Lobster.* c. 1645–50. Oil on canvas, 25 × 33¼″ (64 × 85 cm). Toledo Museum of Art (gift of Edward Drummond Libbey).
b Anthony van Dyck. *Marie-Louise de Tassis.* c. 1630. Oil on canvas. Sammlungen des Regierenden Fürsten von Liechtenstein, Schloss Vaduz.

a

b

a

b

c

Texture

Visual Texture

Trompe-l'œil

The ultimate point in portraying visual texture is called *trompe-l'œil*. A French term meaning "to fool the eye," it is commonly defined as "deceptive painting." In *trompe-l'œil* the objects, in sharp focus, are delineated with meticulous care. The artist copies the exact visual color and value pattern of each surface. A deception occurs, because the appearance of objects is *so* skillfully reproduced that we are momentarily fooled. We look closer even though our rational brain identifies the image as just a painting and not the actual objects.

William Harnett, a 19th-century American artist, is a well-known practitioner of trompe-l'œil painting. Example **a** is especially confusing. A lithographic reproduction of Harnett's famous painting *The Old Violin* has been framed in wood with actual hinges and hardware continuing the painted forms. Separating reality and illusion becomes an entertaining problem for the viewer.

Both **a** and **b**, the latter a painting by Charles King, illustrate a point to remember. The great trompe-l'œil paintings are not famous for this factor of deception alone. The apparently casual arrangement is discovered to be a very carefully planned and balanced pattern of textures, colors, and values. This composition is appreciated longer than our initial amazement at the artist's technical facility.

Example **c** illustrates an amusing extension of the illusion. Here the carefully rendered papers are covered by a piece of broken "glass," which proves to be merely painted also.

Interest in trompe-l'œil has revived along with the general trend back to naturalism in contemporary art. Example **d** is a painting by the American artist Paul Sarkisian. The unusual composition of the meticulously rendered envelopes shows a modern usage of the trompe-l'œil technique.

a William Harnett. *The Old Violin*. 1886. Lithographic reproduction by Gus Ilg, 1887, with frame in three dimensions, 42¾ × 31¾" (109 × 81 cm). Philadelphia Museum of Art.
b Charles Bird King. *The Poor Artist's Cupboard*. c. 1815. Oil on panel, 29¾ × 27¾" (76 × 70 cm). Corcoran Gallery of Art, Washington, D.C.
c Laurent Dabos. *Peace Treaty Between France and Spain*. Oil on canvas, 23 × 18" (59 × 46 cm). Musée Marmottan, Paris.
d Paul Sarkisian. *Untitled*. 1976. Acrylic on paper, 28 × 36" (71 × 91 cm). Courtesy Nancy Hoffman Gallery, New York.

d

Texture

It would be difficult to draw any strict line between *texture* and *pattern.* We immediately associate the word pattern with printed fabrics such as plaids, stripes, polka dots, and floral "patterns." *Pattern* is usually defined as a repetitive design with the same motif appearing again and again. Texture, too, often repeats, but with variations that do not involve such perfect regularity. This difference in the two terms is often slight. A material like burlap would readily be identified as a tactile texture, yet the surface is repetitive enough to be termed a pattern.

The essential distinction between texture and pattern seems to be whether the surface evokes our sense of touch or merely provides designs appealing to the eye. While not mechanically repetitive, the designs dominating the portrait by Klimt in **a** would clearly be termed pattern rather than texture. They do not appeal to our sense of touch but instead create decorative colored figures—literally surface patterns. The naturalistically rendered body emerging from the ornate, flat, patterned surface provides a startling contrast.

The interlocking jigsaw-puzzle shapes of Dubuffet's painting **(b)** produce a busy design of contrasting patterns, not textures.

a Gustav Klimt. *Portrait of Frau Adele Bloch-Bauer.* 1907.
Oil on canvas, 44⅝″ (140 cm) square.
Österreichische Galerie, Vienna.
b Jean Dubuffet. *Nimble Free Hand (Mouchon Berloque).* 1964.
Acrylic on canvas, 4′11″ × 6′7″ (1.5 × 2.01 m).
Tate Gallery, London.

a

b

Color

a

Color

Color has a basic, instinctive visual appeal. Studies have shown repeatedly that we will automatically give our attention to an image in color over one in black and white. Certainly great art has been created without color, but few artists have ignored the added visual interest that color lends. The uninhibited use of color has been a primary characteristic of art in this century. Indeed, our world today is marked by the bold use of color. It could be said we are in the midst of a color revolution. After all, it was not too long ago: that businessmen wore only white shirts, and brown suits were considered too informal for city wear; that "tasteful" living rooms were ecru, brown, and tan with a maroon chair for the color accent; and that the all-white kitchen more closely resembled a hospital operating room than a friendly gathering place. In this vein, too, was Henry Ford's famous remark that the public could have any color Ford car it wanted, as long as it was black.

We certainly are living in a more colorful world than we did in the 30s and 40s. Color, and increasingly vivid color, is found in ever new areas. The public has enthusiastically purchased colored bathtubs, bed linens, and bank checks, colored fry pans and refrigerators, colored pup tents, tissue, tools, and telephones. Fashion design reflects this same fascination with color; even men now have a veritable rainbow of choices when selecting clothes. Today, color appears in factories and office spaces, with the added development of boldly colored supergraphics **(a)** as a reaction against the often drab work areas of the recent past. Science and technology have played a large part in this increasingly colorful world as new materials, new dyes, and new pigments have been developed. We delight in color everywhere.

a Supergraphic for County Federal Savings Bank, Wilton, Conn. 1972. Mary Ann Rumney, designer, for Moore Grover Harper.

Color

Color theory is an extremely complex science. A thorough study of such factors as the various light wavelengths of different colors or the color/heat relationship is interesting but complicated and goes beyond our concern here.

For artists, the essential fact of color theory is that color is a property of *light,* not of an object itself. This property of light was illustrated by Sir Isaac Newton in the 17th century when he put white light through a prism **(a)**. The prism broke up white light into the familiar rainbow of hues. Objects have no color of their own, but have merely the ability to reflect certain rays of white light, which contains all the colors. Blue objects absorb all the rays except the blue ones, and these are reflected to our eyes. Black objects *absorb* all the rays; white objects *reflect* all of them. The significance for the artist in this fact is that, as light changes, color will change. Thus, there is no one objective color for any thing or object.

Related to this same idea, one other color phenomenon is important. Colors change according to their surroundings. Even in the same light, a color will appear different depending on the colors that are adjacent to it. Rarely do we see a color by itself. Perhaps an occasional room or a certain stage set presents just one color, but this is unusual. Normally, colors are seen in conjunction with others and the visual differences are often amazing. A change in value (dark and light) is a common occurrence. Example **b** shows the effect as a green square with its value (darkness or lightness) held constant appears much lighter on the black background than against the white. Example **c** illustrates that even the color effect changes. The small red-purple squares are identical; the differences are caused by the various background colors they are placed against.

a A ray of white light projected through a prism separates into the hues seen in a rainbow.
b When colors are seen in conjunction with one another, they appear to change in value.
c The red-purple squares, although seemingly different, are in fact identical.

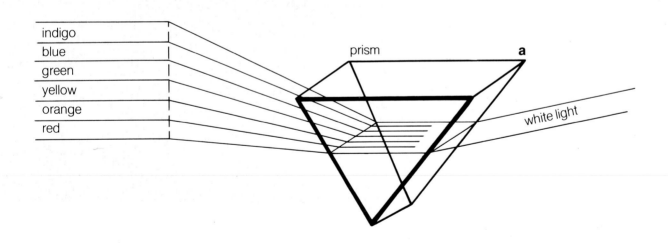

indigo
blue
green
yellow
orange
red

prism   **a**

white light

b

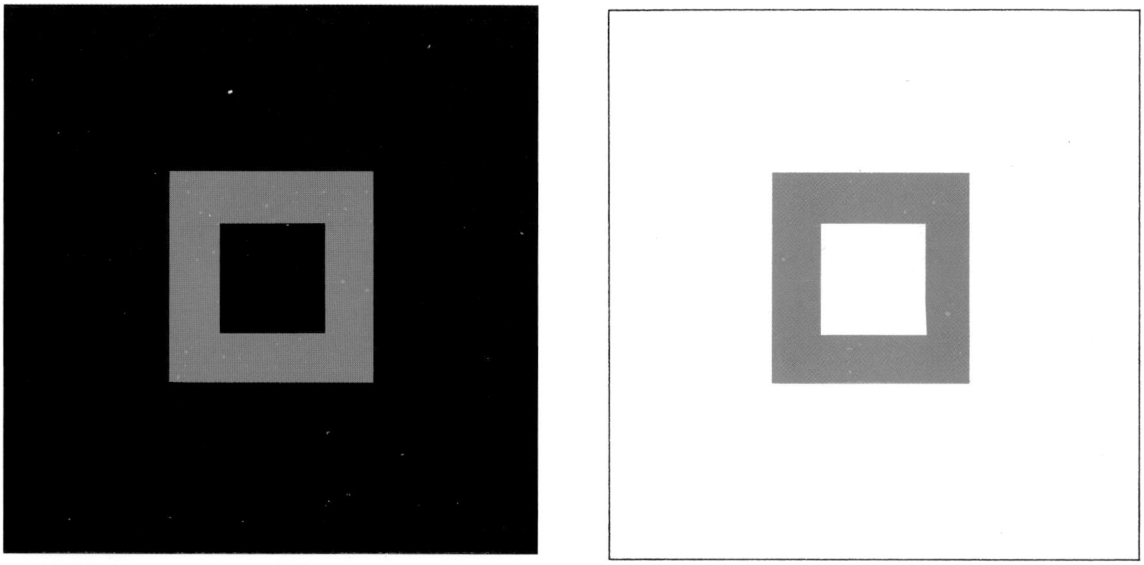

c

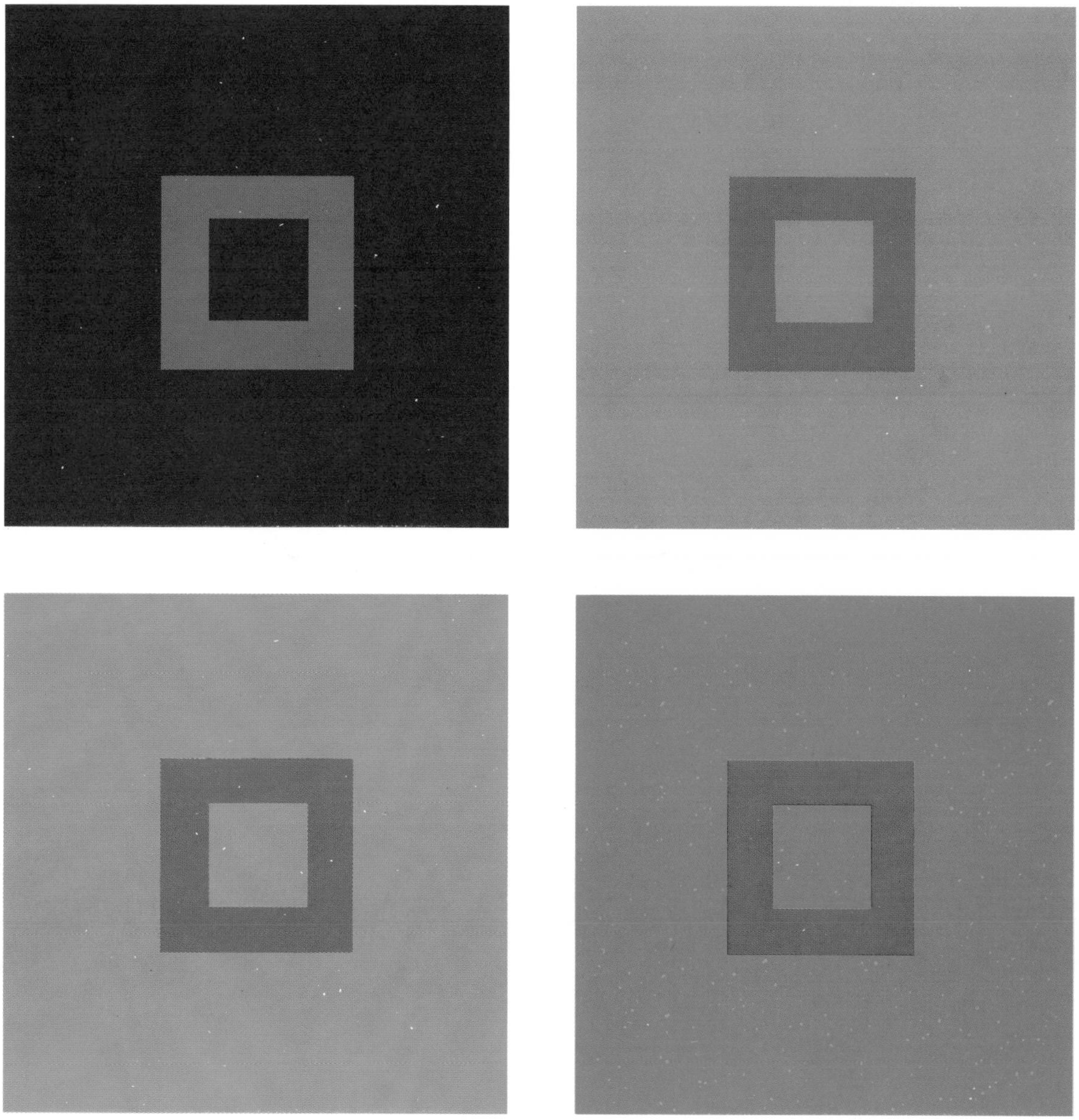

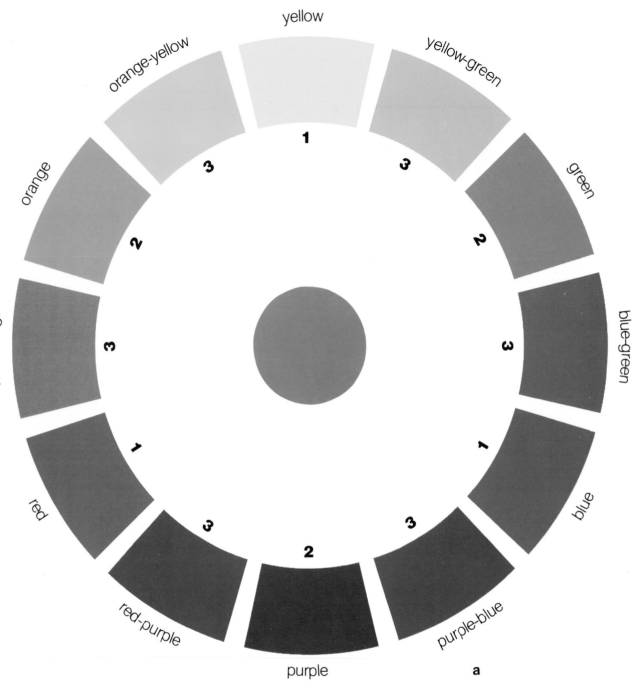

yellow

orange-yellow

yellow-green

orange

green

red-orange

blue-green

red

blue

red-purple

purple-blue

purple

1

3

3

2

2

3

3

1

1

3

2

3

a

Color

Hue

The first property of color is what we call *hue*. Hue simply refers to the name of the color. Red, orange, green, purple, and so forth are hues. There are relatively few actual color names. Confusion exists because in the world of commercial products color names abound: Plum, Adobe, Colonial Blue, Desert Sunset, Mayan Gold, Avocado, and so many more. These often romantic images are extremely inexact terms that mean only what the manufacturers think they mean.

Example **a** shows what is called a *color wheel*—the most common organization of the basic colors. The wheel system dates back to the early 18th century. This particular organization uses twelve hues, which are divided into three categories:

- The three *primary* **(1)** colors are red, yellow, and blue. From these all others are mixed.
- The three *secondary* **(2)** colors are mixtures of the two primaries: red and yellow make orange, yellow and blue make green, blue and red make purple.
- The six *tertiary* **(3)** colors are mixtures of a primary and an adjacent secondary: blue and green make blue-green, red and purple make red-purple, and so on.

It should be noted that this color wheel applies to *pigment*, not *light*. In combining various colors of light, resulting hues could be entirely different from these illustrated here.

This layout of twelve hues is, of course, purely arbitrary, as is this choice of primary colors. Two other color systems are shown just for comparison. Example **b** diagrams the Munsell color organization, **c** the Ostwald wheel. Both of these cite different primary colors. The Munsell system involves the five primaries shown, with five "intermediates" (that is, red plus yellow does not produce "orange" but the intermediate "yellow-red") and a complete wheel of one hundred hues. The Ostwald wheel is based on four primaries, with a total of 24 hues on the complete wheel. All these color organizations are satisfactory, although one or another might be preferred for a specific color problem. This book will use the basic twelve-color wheel, because it works perfectly well for most design problems involving the usual pigment or dye.

a Color wheel showing primary, secondary, and tertiary colors.
b The Munsell color system.
c The Ostwald color system.

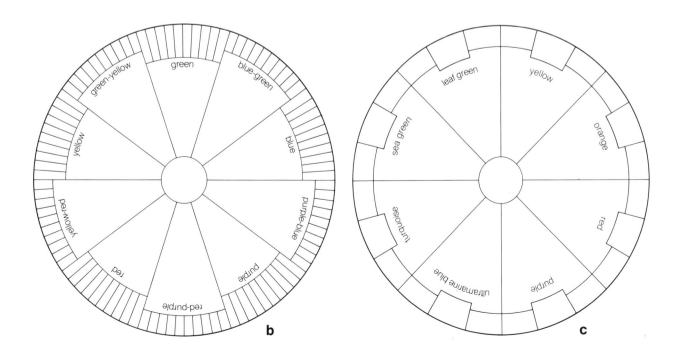

b

c

Color

Value

The second property of color is *value,* which refers to the lightness or darkness of the hue. Example **a** shows a value scale of blue: only one hue is present, but the blue varies widely in light and dark. In pigment, value can be altered by adding white or black paint to the color. Adding white lightens the color and produces a *tint* or high-value color. Adding black darkens the color and produces a *shade* or low-value color. Individual perception varies, but most people can distinguish at least forty tints and shades of any color.

As you can see, not all the colors on the color wheel (p. 216) are shown at the same value. Each is shown at *normal* value, the pure color unmixed and undiluted. The normal values of yellow and of blue, for example, are radically different. Since yellow is a light or high-value color, a yellow value scale would show many more shades than tints. The blue scale here

shows more tints, since normal blue is darker than middle value.

In describing paintings or designs, we often speak of their *value pattern.* This refers to the arrangement and the amount of variation in light and dark, independent of the actual colors. Monet's painting of a figure in a landscape appears in color in **b**. The colors provide sparkle and great visual interest. However, reproduced in black and white **(c)**, with all the colors now translated to values of gray, the painting reveals little value change. The value pattern is almost monotonous. This is rare; most artists are as concerned with the value pattern as with sheer arrangement of colors.

a Value scale of blue.
b Claude Monet. *Madame Monet Under the Willows.* 1880. Oil on canvas, 31⅛ × 23⅝″ (81 × 60 cm). National Gallery of Art, Washington, D.C. (Chester Dale Collection, 1969).
c When Monet's painting **(b)** is reproduced in black and white, there is little contrast in the value pattern.

a

b

c

Color

Intensity / Complementary Colors

The third property of color is called *intensity,* which refers to the brightness of a color. Since a color is at full intensity only when pure and unmixed, there is a relationship between *value* and *intensity.* Mixing black or white with a color changes its value, but at the same time it also affects its intensity. To see the distinction between the two terms, look at **a**. This example shows two tints (high-value) of red. They are about the same degree of lightness, yet one might be called "rose," the other "shocking pink." The two colors are very different in their visual effect, and that difference comes from brightness or intensity. Intensity is sometimes called *chroma* or *saturation.*

There are two ways to lower the intensity of a color—that is, to make a color less bright, more neutral and dull. One way is to mix gray with the color. You can dull a color without changing its value depending on the gray used. The second way is to mix a color with its *complement,* the color directly across from it on the color wheel. Example **b** shows an intensity scale involving the complementary colors blue and orange. Neutralized (low-intensity) versions of a color are often called *tones.* Here we see 3 tones of blue and 3 tones of orange. As progressively more orange is added to the blue, the blue becomes duller, more grayed. The same is true of the orange, which becomes more brown as blue is added. When complements are mixed in equal amounts, they cancel each other out, and a muddy neutral tone is the result.

Complementary colors are direct opposites in position and in character. Mixing complementary colors together dulls them, but when complementary colors are placed *next to each other,* they intensify the brightness of each other. When blue and orange are side by side, each color will appear brighter than in any other context. This effect is called *simultaneous contrast,* meaning that each complement simultaneously intensifies the visual brilliance of the other. Artists make use of this visual effect when they wish to produce brilliant color effects. The marvelous Art Nouveau tapestry in **c** effectively employs complementary colors. Here weirdly flowing red shapes of the angels' dresses contrast with the flat areas of grass in complementary green. The small, round purple shapes of the far background trees stand out vividly against the complementary yellow sky.

One other peculiar visual phenomenon of complementary colors is called *afterimage.* Stare at an area of intense color for a minute or so, and then glance away at a white piece of paper or wall. Suddenly, an area of the complementary color will seem to appear. For example, after staring at a red shape, when you look away at the white wall a definite green area in the same shape will seem to take form on the wall.

a Two tints of red at the same value have different intensities.
b One way to lower the intensity of a color is to mix it with its complement.
c Henri van de Velde. *Engelwache (Angel Vigil).* 1893. Tapestry, 4'6⅜" × 7'6⅞" (1.4 × 2.33 m). Kunstgewerbe Museum, Zurich.

a

b

c

a

b

c

Color

Color and Space

There is a direct relationship between color and a visual impression of depth, or pictorial space. Colors have an innate advancing or receding quality because of slight muscular reactions in our eyes as we focus on different colors. Intense, warm colors (red, orange, yellow) seem to come forward; cool colors (blue, green) seem to go back. In addition, the dust in our atmosphere breaks up the color rays from distant objects and makes them appear bluish. As objects recede, any brilliance of color becomes more neutral, finally seeming to be gray-blue.

Artists can use color's spatial properties to create either an illusion of depth or instead a flat, one-dimensional pattern. The Durand landscape **(a)** gives a feeling of great distance. The overlapping planes of the hills become gradually grayer and more bluish in color as they extend far back from the figures in the foreground. In contrast, Bonnard in his painting **(b)** shows the central background hill as a brilliant, advancing orange that denies the implicit depth and creates a flatter decorative effect.

Even in a still-life painting the spatial quality can be emphasized or ignored. In **c** de Heem

has played up a feeling of depth. While the bright reds and yellows of the fruit tend to advance, the neutral browns and grays of the wall recede. To heighten this effect, the artist gives us a glimpse of landscape through a window, extending far back in grayish blues. On the other hand, Matisse in his still-life **(d)** consciously flattens and compresses space by the use of brilliant, warm colors and strong dark and light value patterns in background areas that would ordinarily recede. An exuberant but very flat painting results.

Examples illustrating the effect of color *value* on an illusion of space will be found in the section "Aerial Perspective" (pp. 100–101).

---

a Asher Durand. *Kindred Spirits*. 1849. Oil on canvas, 46 × 36″ (117 × 92 cm). New York Public Library (Astor, Lenox, and Tilden Foundations).
b Pierre Bonnard. *Mediterranean Coast*. c. 1943. Oil on canvas, 37¾ × 28½″ (96 × 72 cm). Collection Phillips Family.
c Jan Davidsz. de Heem. *Still Life with a View of Antwerp*. 1646. Oil on canvas, 23⅜ × 36½″ (59 × 93 cm). Toledo Museum of Art (gift of Edward Drummond Libbey).
d Henri Matisse. *Still Life in the Studio, Interior at Nice*. 1924. Oil on canvas, 30¾ × 31½″ (76 × 80 cm). Courtesy Marlborough Fine Art Ltd., London.

d

Color

Monochromatic, Analogous, Complementary, Triadic

There are four basic color harmonies (or color *schemes* as they are often called).

A monochromatic harmony involves the use of only one hue. The hue can vary in value, and pure black or white may be added. The visual effect is, of course, extremely harmonious and generally quiet, restful, and (depending on the range of values) subtle.

An analogous harmony combines several colors that sit next to each other on the color wheel. Again, the hues may vary in value. Example **a**, an Impressionist painting by Monet, shows the related harmonious feeling that analogous color lends to a painting.

A complementary harmony, as the term implies, joins colors opposite each other on the color wheel. This combination will produce a lively, exciting pattern, especially with the colors at full intensity. The blue and orange in Davis' painting **(b)** bring a vibrant contrast of color, more dynamic than that in **a**.

A triadic harmony involves three hues equally spaced on the color wheel. Red, yellow, and blue would be the most common example **(c)**. Since the hues come from different parts of the wheel, the result is again contrasting and lively.

These harmonies are probably more applicable to such design areas as interiors, posters, pack-aging, and the like than to painting. In painting, color is used intuitively, and artists rarely work by formula. But knowing these harmonies can be helpful to designers in consciously planning the visual effects they wish a finished pattern to have. Moreover, color can easily provide a visual unity that perhaps was not obvious in the initial pattern of shapes. While design aims vary, often the more complicated and "busy" the pattern of shapes, the more useful will be a strict control of the color—and the reverse.

Color unity is described by another term. We often speak of the *tonality* of a design or painting. Tonality refers to the dominance of a single color or the visual importance of a hue that seems to pervade the whole color structure despite the presence of other colors. Monochromatic patterns, of course, give a uniform tonality, since only one hue is present. Analogous color schemes can also produce a dominant tonality, as **a** shows. When colors are chosen from one part of the color wheel, they will share one hue in common. Yellow-green, blue-green, blue, and blue-purple all derive from the primary blue, so they yield a *blue tonality* in this work.

a Claude Monet. *Palazzo da Mula, Venice.* 1908. Oil on canvas, 24½ × 32″ (62 × 81 cm). National Gallery of Art, Washington, D.C. (Chester Dale Collection).
b Stuart Davis. *Colonial Cubism.* 1954. Oil on canvas, 3′9″ × 5′⅛″ (1.14 × 1.53 m). Walker Art Center, Minneapolis (gift of T. B. Walker Foundation).
c Pablo Picasso. *Mandolin and Guitar.* 1924. Oil with sand on canvas, 4′7⅜″ × 6′6⅛″ (1.41 × 2 m). Solomon R. Guggenheim Museum, New York.

a

b

c

Color

Discord

Color *discord* is the opposite of color harmony. A combination of discordant colors is visually disturbing, for the colors have no basic affinity for each other. They seem to clash, to be pulling away in opposing directions rather than relating harmoniously to one another. The term "discord" conveys an immediate negative impression. Discord in life, in a personal relationship, may certainly not be pleasant, but it often provides excitement. In the same manner, discord can be extremely useful in art and design.

Mild discord results in exciting, eye-catching color combinations. The world of fashion has exploited the idea to the point that mildly discordant combinations are almost commonplace. A discordant color note in a painting or design may contribute visual surprise and also perhaps better express certain themes or ideas. A poster could attract attention by its startling colors.

At one time rules were taught about just which color combinations were harmonious and which were definitely to be avoided because the colors did not "go together." A combination of pink and orange was unthinkable; even blue and green patterns were suspect. Today, of course, these rules seem silly, and we approach color more freely, seeking out unexpected combinations.

Colors widely separated on the color wheel (but *not* complements) are generally seen as discordant combinations. The following combinations will produce visual discord and are illustrated here.

- Example **a** combines a primary and a tertiary beyond an adjacent secondary: red and blue-purple.
- Example **b** combines a secondary and a tertiary beyond an adjacent primary: orange and yellow-green.
- Example **c** combines two tertiaries on either side of a primary: blue-green and blue-purple.

In producing discord, value is an important consideration. As **d** shows, the impression of discord is much greater when the value of the two colors is similar. With great dark and light contrast between the hues, few color combinations will look truly unpleasant. But when the value contrast is absent, we begin to see the actual disharmony of the hues.

The painting by Franz Marc **(e)** has many areas where purposely discordant colors are placed together. Hence, the effect is visually unsettling.

a Red and blue-purple.
b Orange and yellow-green.
c Blue-green and blue-purple.
d Pure orange and two shades of blue-purple.
e Franz Marc. *The Yellow Cow.* 1911.
  Oil on canvas, 4'7⅜ × 6'2½" (1.41 × 1.89 m).
  Solomon R. Guggenheim Museum, New York.

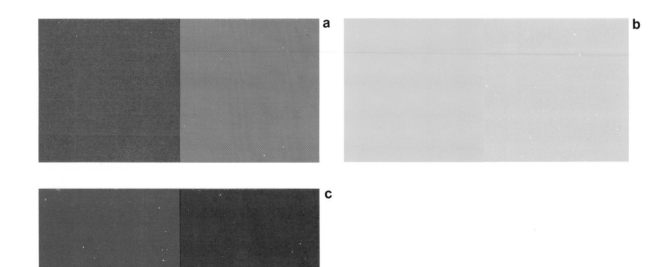

d

e

Color

There are three basic ways in which color can be used in painting.

When artists reproduce the colors seen in nature, colors seen by white daylight, they are said to be using *local color*. Grass is green, the sky blue, apples red. The colors are the ones we customarily think objects to be. The artist controls the color scheme, but primarily by the choice of subject matter. This color use is also sometimes termed *objective* color.

Artists who use *optical color* again reproduce the visual image. They paint the colors they see, but in this case under illumination other than natural white daylight. Since color is a property of light, the colors of objects change at sunset, under moonlight, by candlelight as in **a**, or even by incandescent lamplight.

In *arbitrary color,* natural colors are ignored. The artist's color choices are based purely on aesthetic or emotional reasons. The colors in Derain's painting **(b)** were chosen for their brilliance and lively contrast, not for any descriptive reference to the natural colors of the London scene. Arbitrary color is sometimes difficult to pinpoint, because many painters took some artistic liberties in using color. Even in works by the Impressionists, whose overriding interest was optical color, the *heightened* color effects could often be termed arbitrary **(c)**. Arbitrary color is most clearly seen in 20th-century painting. Just as art in general has moved away from naturalism, so has arbitrary color tended to become the primary interest. Even color photography, with filters, infrared film, and various darkroom techniques, has experimented widely in arbitrary color effects.

These categories of color use obviously apply to paintings with identifiable subject matter. In nonobjective art the forms have no reference to natural objects, so the color, too, is nonobjective. Purely aesthetic considerations determine the color choices.

a Georges de la Tour. *The Repentant Magdalen.* c. 1640. Oil on canvas, 14½ × 36½″ (37 × 93 cm). National Gallery of Art, Washington, D.C. (Ailsa Mellon Bruce Fund).
b André Derain. *London Bridge.* 1906. Oil on canvas, 26 × 39″ (66 × 99 cm). Museum of Modern Art, New York (gift of Mr. and Mrs. Charles Zadok).
c Claude Monet. *Poplars on the Bank of the Epte River.* 1891. Oil on canvas, 39½ × 25¾″ (100 × 65 cm). Philadelphia Museum of Art (bequest of Anne Thomson as a Memorial to her Father, Frank Thomson, and her Mother, Mary Elizabeth Clarke Thomson).

b

c

Color

"Ever since our argument, I've been *blue*."
"I saw *red* when she lied to me."
"You're certainly in a *black* mood today."
"I was *green* with envy when I saw their
new house."

These statements are emotional. We are expressing an emotional reaction, and somehow a color reference makes the meaning clearer, since color does appeal to our emotions and feelings. For artists who wish to arouse an emotional response in the viewer, color is the most effective element. Even before we "read" the subject matter or identify the forms, the color has already created an atmosphere to which we have responded.

In a very elemental instance, we commonly recognize so-called warm and cool colors. Yellows, oranges, and reds give us an instinctive feeling of warmth and hence evoke warm, happy, cheerful reactions. Cooler blues and greens are automatically associated with more quiet, less outgoing feelings and can express melancholy or depression. These are generalities, of course, for the combination of colors is vital. Also, the artist can influence our reactions by the values and intensities of the colors selected.

Paintings in which color causes an emotional reaction and relates to the thematic subject matter are very common. But notice the difference that color *alone* can make in our emotional reaction to a painting. Examples **a** and **b** are nonobjective; there is *no* subject matter. Yet what a different feeling each work gives us because of the color choices. The complementary blue and orange in Hofmann's painting **(a)** are vibrantly alive. These clean, sparkling bright colors have a cheerful, pleasant effect. By contrast, the reddish brown overlaid with foreboding heavy strokes of black seen in Soulages' *Peinture 7 Nov. 59* **(b)** arouse a totally different emotional feeling.

It is interesting to note how the feeling of shape can be related to color. A jagged, angular, dynamic shape in a soft grayish blue can seem like a design contradiction. It is generally more satisfactory to select colors that relate to the already present emotional qualities of the shapes (or the reverse). All elements of a design should work together unless a deliberate incongruity (and visual confusion) is the desired effect.

a Hans Hofmann. *The Golden Wall*. 1961. Oil on canvas, 5′ × 6′½″ (1.5 × 1.84 m). Art Institute of Chicago (Mr. and Mrs. Frank G. Logan Prize Fund).
b Pierre Soulages. *Peinture 7 Nov. 59*. 1959. Oil on canvas, 4′6¼″ × 2′11″ (1.38 × .89 m). Courtesy Gimpel & Weitzenhoffer Ltd., New York.

Color

"Don't worry, he's true *blue*."
"I caught him *red*-handed."
"So I told her a little *white* lie."
"Why not just admit you're too *yellow* to do it?"

We frequently utter statements that employ color references to describe character traits or human behavior. These color references are *symbolic*. Here the colors symbolize abstract concepts or ideas: fidelity, sin, innocence, and cowardice. The colors do not stand for tangibles like fire, grass, water, or even sunlight. They represent mental, conceptual qualities. The particular colors chosen to symbolize various ideas are often arbitrary or the initial reasons so buried in history we no longer remember them. Can we really explain why green means "go" and red signifies "stop"?

A main point to remember is that symbolic color references are cultural; they are not worldwide but vary from one society to another. What color is the color of mourning that one associates with a funeral? Our society would say black, but the answer would be white in India, violet in Turkey, brown in Ethiopia, and yellow in Burma. What is the color of royalty? We think of purple (dating back to the Egyptians), but the royal color was yellow in dynastic China and red in ancient Rome (which has perservered in the Cardinals' robes of the Catholic Church). What does a bride wear? White is our response, but yellow is the choice in India as it was in Rome. Different eras and different cultures invent different color symbols.

The symbolic use of color was very important in ancient art for identifying specific figures or deities to an illiterate public. Not only the ancients, however, used color in this manner. In countless pictures of the Virgin Mary through centuries of Western art, it is very rare that she is not shown in a blue robe over a red or white dress.

Symbolic color designations are less important in art than they once were. Still, they linger on and can be helpful to an artist in creating designs on specific themes. Often, art's purpose is the communication of ideas. Bravery or courage *can* be expressed visually without the use of red, but why attempt it if that is the commonly associated color reference (and the most recognizable) in most of the viewers' minds?

Bibliography

Art History

Arnason, H. H. *History of Modern Art,* 2nd ed. Englewood Cliffs, N.J.: Prentice-Hall, 1976.

Elsen, Albert E. *Purposes of Art,* 3rd ed. New York: Holt, Rinehart & Winston, 1972.

Janson, H. W. *History of Art,* 2nd ed. New York: Prentice-Hall and Harry N. Abrams, Inc., 1977.

General Design

Anderson, Donald M. *Elements of Design.* New York: Holt, Rinehart & Winston, 1961.

Bevlin, Marjorie Elliott. *Design Through Discovery,* 3rd ed. New York: Holt, Rinehart & Winston, 1977.

Bothwell, Dorr, and Marlyn Frey. *Notan: The Dark-Light Principle of Design.* New York: Van Nostrand Reinhold, 1976.

Collier, Graham. *Form, Space and Vision.* Englewood Cliffs, N.J.: Prentice-Hall, 1967.

De Lucio-Meyer, J. *Visual Aesthetics.* New York: Harper and Row, 1974.

De Sausmarez, Maurice. *Basic Design: The Dynamics of Visual Form.* New York: Van Nostrand Reinhold, 1975.

Faulkner, Ray, and Edwin Zeigfeld. *Art Today,* 5th ed. New York: Holt, Rinehart & Winston, 1969.

Hale, Nathan Cabot. *Abstraction in Art and Nature.* New York: Watson-Guptill Publications, 1972.

Harlan, Calvin. *Vision and Invention: A Course in Art Fundamentals.* Englewood Cliffs, N.J.: Prentice-Hall, 1970.

Henri, Robert. *The Art Spirit.* New York: J. B. Lippincott Co., 1960.

Hurlburt, Allen. *Layout: The Design of the Printed Page.* New York: Watson-Guptill Publications, 1977.

Itten, Johannes. *Design and Form,* 2nd rev. ed. New York: Van Nostrand Reinhold, 1976.

Kepes, Gyorgy. *Language of Vision.* Chicago: Paul Theobald, 1969.

Knobler, Nathan. *The Visual Dialogue,* 2nd ed. New York: Holt, Rinehart & Winston, 1971.

Lowry, Bates. *The Visual Experience,* 2nd ed. Englewood Cliffs, N.J.: Prentice-Hall, 1975.

Maier, Manfred. *Basic Principles of Design.* New York: Van Nostrand Reinhold, 1977.

Mante, Harald. *Photo Design: Picture Composition for Black and White Photography.* New York: Van Nostrand Reinhold, 1971.

Ocvirk, Otto G., Robert O. Bone, Robert E. Stinson, and Philip R. Wigg. *Art Fundamentals: Theory and Practice,* 3rd ed. Dubuque, Iowa: William Brown, 1975.

Weismann, Donald L. *The Visual Arts as Human Experience.* Englewood Cliffs, N.J.: Prentice-Hall, 1970.

Wong, Wucius. *Principles of Two-Dimensional Design.* New York: Van Nostrand Reinhold, 1972.

Visual Perception

Arnheim, Rudolf. *Art and Visual Perception: A Psychology of the Creative Eye.* Berkeley: University of California Press, 1974.

Ehrenzweig, Anton. *The Hidden Order of Art.* Berkeley: University of California Press, 1976.

Gombrich, E. H. *Art and Illusion: A Study in the Psychology of Pictorial Representation.* Princeton, N.J.: Princeton University Press, 1961.

Space

Carraher, Ronald G., and Jacqueline B. Thurston. *Optical Illusions and the Visual Arts.* New York: Van Nostrand Reinhold, 1966.

D'Amelio, Joseph. *Perspective Drawing Handbook.* New York: Leon Amiel, Publisher, 1964.

Doblin, Jay. *Perspective: A New System for Designers,* 11th ed. New York: Whitney Library of Design, 1976.

Held, Richard, editor. *Image, Object, and Illusion,* readings from *Scientific American.* San Francisco: W. H. Freeman and Co., 1974.

Ivins, William M. *On the Rationalization of Sight.* New York: Da Capo Press, 1973.

Luckiesh, M. *Visual Illusions: Their Causes, Characteristics and Applications.* New York: Dover Publications, 1965.

Mulvey, Frank. *Graphic Perception of Space.* New York: Van Nostrand Reinhold, 1969.

Pevsner, Nikolaus. *An Outline of European Architecture.* New York: Penguin Books, 1970.

Pirenne, M. H. *Optics, Painting and Photography.* Cambridge: Cambridge University Press, 1970.

Walters, Nigel V., and John Bromham. *Principles of Perspective.* New York: Watson-Guptill Publication, 1974.

White, J. *The Birth and Rebirth of Pictorial Space,* 2nd ed. New York: Harper and Row, 1973.

Texture

Battersby, Marton. *Trompe-L'œil: The Eye Deceived.* New York: St. Martin's Press, 1974.

Brodatz, Phil. *Textures: A Photographic Album for Artists and Designers.* New York: Dover, 1966.

Janis, Harriet, and Rudi Blesh. *Collage: Personalities, Concepts, Techniques,* rev. ed. Philadelphia: Chilton

Book Co., 1967.

Proctor, Richard M. *The Principles of Pattern: For Craftsmen and Designers.* New York: Van Nostrand Reinhold, 1969.

Wescher, Herta. *Collage.* New York: Harry N. Abrams, 1968.

Color

Albers, Josef. *Interaction of Color,* rev. ed. New Haven, Conn.: Yale University Press, 1972.

Birren, Faber. *Color: A Survey in Words and Pictures from Ancient Mysticism to Modern Science.* New York: University Books, 1962.

———. *Principles of Color.* New York: Van Nostrand Reinhold, 1969.

———, editor. *Itten: The Elements of Color.* New York: Van Nostrand Reinhold, 1970.

———, editor. *Munsell: A Grammar of Color.* New York: Van Nostrand Reinhold, 1969.

———. *Ostwald: The Color Primer.* New York: Van Nostrand Reinhold, 1969.

Fabri, Frank. *Color: A Complete Guide for Artists.* New York: Watson-Guptill Publications, 1967.

Gerritsen, Frank J. *Theory and Practice of Color.* New York: Van Nostrand Reinhold, 1974.

Itten, Johannes. *The Art of Color.* New York: Van Nostrand Reinhold, 1974.

Küppers, Harald. *Color: Origin, Systems, Uses.* New York: Van Nostrand Reinhold, 1973.

Rhode, Ogden N. *Modern Chromatics: The Student's Textbook of Color with Application to Art and Industry,* new ed. New York: Van Nostrand Reinhold, 1973.

Index

Photographic Sources

Photographic source references are to page number followed by illustration letter.

Agraci-Art Reference Bureau, Ancram, N.Y. (11c); Alinari-Art Reference Bureau, Ancram, N.Y. (14a, 36a, 68a, 73b, 78a, 91b, 92c, 103d, 129d, 133d, 165b, 176a); Alinari-Scala/EPA, New York (110a); Anderson-Art Reference Bureau, Ancram, N.Y. (40b, 42a, 109c, 178a); © Archives Photographiques, Paris (124a, 126a); Australian Information Service, New York (144b); Oliver Baker, New York (175d); E. Irving Blomstrann, New Britain, Conn. (48b); Brenwasser, New York (105c); Brogi-Art Reference Bureau, Ancram, N.Y. (86a); Bruckmann-Art Reference Bureau, Ancram, N.Y. (61e); Bulloz, Paris (175b); Rudolph Burckhardt, New York (185b); R. Camprubi, Barcelona (198a); Leo Castelli Gallery, New York (32a, 165c); Geoffrey Clements, Staten Island, N.Y. (23b, 29b, 43c, 117d, 181c, 194a); Bevan Davies, New York (207d); Russell Dian, New York (3a, 4a, 4b, 152b); Terry Dintenfass Gallery, New York (145c); Robert Doisneau, Paris (60a); English Life Publications, Ltd., Derby (17d); Foto Rossi (42b); Fotostudio Otto, Vienna (146a, 208a); Fototeca Unione, Rome (128b); Alison Frantz, Princeton, N.J. (83b, 144a); Ann Freedman, Emmerich Gallery, New York (115e); Frequin-Photos, Voorburg, The Netherlands (158a); Galerie Daber, Paris (161e); George Gardner, Belle Harbor, N.Y. (106a, 106b); Giraudon, Paris (25c, 30b, 46a, 52c, 57c, 68b, 117b, 157e, 193d); Raccolta G. Grassi, Milan (133c); Hedrich-Blessing, Chicago (18b); Brughard Hofer (185c); A. F. Kersting, London (14b, 40d); Library of Congress, Washington, D.C. (40c, 108a, 185d); Magnum, New York (100a, 130a); Marlborough Gallery, Inc., New York (129c); Marlborough Gallery, Inc., New York, and Robert E. Mates, New York (48c); Robert E. Mates, New York (16a); Robert E. Mates, New York, and Mary Donlon (131d); Metropolitan Museum of Art, New York (90a); A. Mirzaoff, Tampa, Fla. (8a); Al Mozell, New York (25d); Museum of Fine Arts, Boston (5c); National Board of Antiquities and Historical Monuments, Helsinki (91c); National Gallery, London (193c); National Tourist Organization of Greece, Athens, and Pavlos Myloff, Athens (15c); Robert Perron, New York (212a); Eric Pollitzer, Hempstead, N.Y. (71b, 113b, 117c); Nathan Rabin, New York (77c); Roger-Viollet, Paris (41e); Georges Routhier, Studio Lourmel 77, Paris (206e); William S. Rubin, New York (19c); Service de Documentation Photographique de la Réunion des Musées Nationaux, Paris (132b, 160a, 191b); Sopraintendenza per i Beni Artistici e Storici, Parma, and Fornari & Ziveri, Parma (107c); Soprintendenza alle Gallerie, Florence (37b, 37c); Ezra Stoller © ESTO, Mamaroneck, N.Y. (45b); Soichi Sunami, New York (9b, 18a, 33b, 76b, 97c, 140a, 165d, 189c); Charles Swedlund, Cobden, Ill. (102a); Joseph Szaszfai, Branford, Conn. (27c, 74a); Svend Thomsen, Hjørring, Denmark (60b); Wolfgang Volz, Essen, West Germany (70a); Walter Wachter (205b); Robert Wallace, Indianapolis, Ind. (182b, 183c); Wildenstein & Co., Inc., New York (222b).

Works by Braque, Calder, Cassatt, Derain, Duchamp, Gris, Kandinsky, Kupka, Lurçat, Magritte, Miró, Soulages, Tàpies: © A.D.A.G.P., Paris, 1978.

Works by Escher, Mondrian: © Beeldrecht, 1978.

Works by Bonnard, Degas, Dufy, Klee, Maillol, Matisse, Monet, Picasso, Renoir, Rodin, Rouault, Schwitters, Soutine, Utrillo, Vasarely; photos by Archives Photographiques: © S.P.A.D.E.M., 1978.

Works by Ernst, Namuth, Rauschenberg: © V.A.G.A., 1978.